D1859712

Rethinking Tourism

Chronicle of a Stormy Journey

Rethinking Tourism

Chronicle of a Stormy Journey

M.P. Bezbaruah

GYAN

Published by

Gyan Publishing House
5, Ansari Road
Daryaganj, New Delhi-110002
Phone: 011-47034999, 9811692060
E-mail: books@gyanbooks.com

Distribution Network
gyanbooks.com
India, USA, Canada, UK, Australia, France

ISBN: 978-93-6280-031-2 (PB)

First Published, 2024

Printed at: Gyan Press, Delhi.

Rethinking Tourism
Author: M.P. Bezbaruah

To

ANU

In memory of the unfinished journey

Contents

Foreword 1

In the early days of the Covid pandemic my longtime friend Madan Bezbaruah – a quiet, globally respected architect of India's renowned tourism, aviation and hospitality sector, wrote the following in one his regular "diary notes"--

"Perhaps it is time to collate the lessons of this pandemic and see if some such plan for automatic disaster management response for the sector which also provides insurance and social security umbrella and income and liquidity support to the most vulnerable sections of the industry could be devised."

He then proceeded to do just that. Including his thoughts on the regulatory and operating frameworks needed to move to the next step. His views, shaped within the Hotel Association of India, are always progressive yet always reasonable. Always balanced between the interests of the Nation, State and Local Community on the one hand and of the industry on the other. Identifying so clearly the missed opportunities and the challenges. Always human and fair at the core.

And he has created a vivid and highly enjoyable story. It is also a lesson on both the rich pageantry of the Indian tourism experience and its very impressive revival from the brink of disaster. It is packed with data and policy concepts that will form a model recovery guide for any future downturn. The analysis is profound and it has sound sustainable development advice, not just for Indian stakeholders, but from a global perspective.

Today India is one of the real hopes for all our futures – embodying the well known "economic powerhouse across the economy" that is Travel & Tourism, but also with its base in the world's largest democracy, it can be a beacon for *how tourism should be operated* – responsive to the existential climate crisis, aligned with the sustainable development goals, and respectful of nature.

In 1972 when my friend and mentor the late Maurice Strong convened the first Earth Summit in Stockholm, only one world leader was present – Indira Gandhi. Strong knew that India was the pivotal player in a world of a small number of richer developed States and the large majority of poorer developing ones.

Today, half a century later, Madan Bezbaruah has chronicled how India can fulfil that pivotal role in the cross cutting tourism and hospitality economy. Powered by booming domestic tourism and poised to strengthen global socio-economic development. This is not only a story about India – it is an object lesson for all of us. And a primer for tomorrow's young leaders around the world.

The last but one chapter on the urgent, priority need to act on the existential climate crisis - which threatens humanity like COVID on steroids - is a clarion call to all of us, everywhere.

Geoffrey Lipman,

May 2024.

President SUN^x Malta. (on Climate Action)
Former - Executive Director IATA:
President WTTC:
Assistant Secretary General UNWTO.

Foreword 2

I got acquainted with Mr. Madan Bezbaruah when he was Secretary of Tourism, Ministry of Tourism, the Government of India. Then I was holding the position of regional director for Asia and the Pacific in the United Nations World Tourism Organization (UNWTO), and developed a close working relationship with this fine gentleman in a vast number of areas of mutual collaboration, which subsequently resulted in the then Secretary-General of UNWTO appointing Madan as the UNWTO Representative in India when he retired.

Now we both are retired for some time. But the bond of relationship continued into that of friendship. I say that Madan is a fine gentleman not because of the official position he held but rather due to his kindness in treating people, be a stranger, a subordinate of his or an external encounter like in my case. His friendliness is intrinsic and comes so naturally when you meet him. I believe this softness of his is not just a consequence of cultivation but rather it must be part of his family genes.

More importantly, Madan is such a refined professional in travel and tourism. His knowledge in the technical field is very awesome. What impressed me the most is the fact that he is always on top of the fast-changing trends and comes up with tailor-made sets of tourism policies for the public as well as for the private sectors.

I am delighted that he has assembled this tourism journey of his into a book, one in which his thoughts and insightfulness have certainly summed up the past of the regional tourism in general and the tourism industry in India in particular. It is definitely a well-orchestrated food for thought for the travel and tourism professionals and also for the general travelling public. I wish Madan all the best both in his continued dedication to work and the enjoyment of retired life.

Xu Jing
Former Regional Director for Asia and the Pacific,
United Nations World Tourism Organization (UNWTO)

Introduction

This book is a collection of many articles written during a period when tourism and hospitality sector were going through an unprecedented crisis due to the Covid 19 pandemic. The articles chronicle the dimensions of the problems as they emerged, the impact on income and employment, the struggle of the industry to stay afloat, the slow process of recovery and the resilience of the industry through the entire period. Most of the articles were written for the Hotel Association of India's (HAI) mouthpiece magazine , ENGAGE, and the others too, in my capacity as the Secretary General of HAI. They reflect therefore the key focus of our advocacy with the government --the importance of tourism as an instrument of inclusive growth or, as the Prime Minister Modi has often declared, as a pillar of development.

Why Tourism?

In the last few years, the UN General Assembly had two unprecedented meetings on the critical role of tourism in advancing sustainable development. In the second thematic meeting the President of the General Assembly Dennis Francis, said "We need a global tourism sector that is sustainable – one with deep local value chains that expand demand for locally made products and services in ways that also directly and positively benefit local communities; a sector that serves as a positive force for biodiversity conservation, heritage protection and climate friendly livelihoods." The Secretary General, UNWTO emphasized "The growing significance of the tourism sector for our societies and our economies brings with it extra responsibility. We cannot allow the lifeline of tourism to be cut again. Resilience in the tourism is not just a matter of planning or reacting to crises. It is also about proactively addressing the underlying factors of those crises. Unsustainable consumption is leading to biodiversity loss, climate change and the emergence of pandemics. It's vital that we adopt policies that accelerate transformative change."[1]

The Osaka Declaration of the G 20 meeting in June 2019 significantly mentions tourism's wide-ranging contributions in –" the creation of quality jobs and entrepreneurship, especially for women and youth and in the creative industry; economic resilience and recovery; the preservation of natural resources through sustainable tourism planning and management; and the achievement of inclusive and sustainable development."

The Goa Roadmap of G 20 in 2023 continued this emphasis on tourism. "The Roadmap also expands on UNWTO's work in placing tourism at the forefront of the global agenda and advancing knowledge on how to design better tourism policies to accelerate the achievement of the SDGs, in particular in the areas of sustainability, destination management, governance, education, innovation, digital transformation and investments."[2]

The total impact of tourism industry has been widely documented but it is best summed up in the words of UNWTO[3] "an economic powerhouse that represents 10% of world GDP, 30% of services exports, and 1 out of every 10 jobs in the world, tourism is the third highest world category in export earnings. As a sector that has inter-linkages with virtually all other economic sectors, tourism produces profound and wide-ranging impacts across all dimensions of sustainable development. Thus, tourism offers significant opportunities as a tool for development, including the prospects it offers for women and youth; its relative importance for developing states, rural areas and indigenous communities; its potential to

1. UN Tourism: UN General Assembly Hosts Tourism for Sustainable Development Event 17 Apr 2024.
2. UNWTO: GOA Roadmap for Tourism as a vehicle for achieving the Sustainable Development Goals. p. 4.
3. UNWTO, Tourism for Development, 2018 p. 29.

incentivize the conservation of environmental resources and cultural assets; and its capacity to spur interaction and understanding."

The multiplier effects of tourism are very high and tourism's indirect and induced contribution is equally impressive. WTTC Travel and Tourism Global Economic impact 2017 estimates the impact to be USD 4.97 trillion, representing 7.1% of global GDP. Indirect contributions include spending on tourism investment (e.g., construction of hotels), domestic purchases by sectors that deal directly with tourists (e.g., purchases of food by hotels) and certain other aspects of government spending. Tourism's induced contribution involves spending by those who are directly or indirectly employed by the tourism sector.

Tourism continued to have its pre-eminent position in the world in respect of contribution to GDP and employment creation. Overcoming the ever-increasing and unpredictable shocks from terrorist attacks and political instability, health pandemics and natural disasters of earlier years, WTTC says, in its annual analysis quantifying the global economic and employment impact of Travel & Tourism in 185 countries and 25 regions, "that the sector accounted for 10.4% of global GDP and 319 million jobs, or 10% of total employment in 2018 and the sector accounted for 6.5% of total global exports and 27.2% of total global service exports."[4] The growth in Travel & Tourism industry sector reaching 3.9%, outpaced the global economic growth of 3.2% for the eighth consecutive year. Generally financial and business services, manufacturing, public services, retail and distribution, and transport sectors are more visible as drivers of economic growth. But in 116 of the 185 countries covered by the annual economic impact research by WTTC in 2018, tourism's performance was stronger than the growth recorded in these sectors.

Covid 19 changed all that. This book is a story of that catastrophe. The pandemic pushed back tourism by 30 years, with staggering impact on jobs, income and GDP of almost all countries. At stake was $1.3 trillion of tourism earnings, global GDP

4. World Travel and Tourism Council (WTTC). 2019. Global Economic Impact and Trends 2019. Foreword and P.5.

loss of $2 trillion and 100-120 million direct jobs. It is also the story of the struggle for recovery and slow resurgence by 2024. The following pages recount all that.

The articles were written as part of my association with the hospitality sector. Therefore, it has much reference to the sector. Some statements and statistics will be repetitive because the articles were written for different journals at different times. I have not tried to edit them or to take them out because that will disturb the flow of the narratives and the context.

Much of the narrative can now be put in the past tense. But I believe the history of global tourism and that of India will be incomplete without a narration of the experience of this unusual time. If even in the slightest way this chronicle helps in future in avoiding the horrible experiences of the pandemic days, my efforts and commitment to tourism would have been amply rewarded.

I am very grateful to my long-time friend Mr. Geoffrey Lipman for so readily agreeing to write the foreword. I have known Mr. Lipman for many years for his pioneering role in many tourism institutions like the WTTC and now Sun X Malta and am amazed by his indefatigable pursuit of sustainable development practices. I am also grateful to my friend Mr. Xu Jing who handled Asia-Pacific region in the UNWTO and was always so helpful, positive and practical in his approach. Their words add value to my book.

I must thank young and energetic MD of Gyan Publishing House, Shri Amit Garg who so readily agreed to continue our long association as the publisher of my earlier four books.

But I ***miss*** what I had during the preparation of those four books--the comforting support, pragmatic counsel and patient editing of my wife Anuradha.

The Gathering Storm

1

TRAVEL IN THE TIME OF CORONAVIRUS[1]

Never before the world has come to a standstill like it has after Covid-19. Never before was travel and tourism so grounded as it is now. The United Nations World Tourism Organisation (UNWTO) reports that 100 percent global destinations now have travel restrictions. From whatever little we know and what all we do not about the Covid -19 virus it is safe to say that it is not going away all too soon. Government, therefore, is engaged in strategy to balance between saving lives now and ensuring that economic collapse do not take more lives in the future.

Many of the economic activities so badly shattered will soon limp back to life. But one of the biggest industry of the world--travel and tourism-- which has been growing faster than the world economy, creating 10 percent of the global workforce and contributing almost 10 percent of global GDP will be unable to take that risk for some more time. The major known weapon to fight Covid-19 social distancing and staying home — is just the antithesis of what makes travel and tourism. Concern for health safety and fear of recurrence may dictate a cautious approach to putting travel and tourism on the rails.

The adverse impact is phenomenal. UNWTO foresees a decline of 20 to 30 percent in tourist arrivals. In 2019, tourism receipts had

1. Print 20 May 2020.

touched $1.5 trillion. In India a recent report has put the possible compression of 70-75 percent of business in the hotel and aviation sector alone. UNWTO admits these are early and tentative estimates. The impact is difficult to estimate as travel and tourism is directly or indirectly comprised of large number of activities and the ripple effects are deep and wide. The informal sector predominates travel and tourism industry. Globally as in India about 80 percent of the industry is composed of small and medium enterprise—not taking into account huge number of craftsmen, artisans and artists in the cultural sector and other service providers who depend on tourism for their day to day existence. They are very vulnerable and every passing day of inactivity pushes them closer to the brink of collapse.

Appropriately, Ministry of Tourism has set up a Task Force for tourism revival. The Task Force has no time to lose to do a few things that need to be done urgently. First, with the assistance of the industry a quick assessment of the ground situation should be made. The Task Force must work out a plan of action for the industry as a whole. However, many of the actions to be taken are likely to be beyond the competence of the Ministry. Therefore, the Ministry should ensure that the plan is made part of the broad national economic recovery plan.

The Task Force may have to go beyond 'revival'. First it should look at the question of 'survival' of large segments of the industry if the reopening takes time as most probably it would. Then to look at 'recovery' of the industry. The support needed perhaps will make a long list but on top of the list will be payroll support, credit guarantee, provision of liquidity, providing benefits of 'industry', rationalisation of GST, review taxes, regulations inhibiting transport and tourism -- just to mention a few. Third, steps for 'revival' of pre-Covid-19 activities and going beyond that for a new future should be the agenda. This will involve incentives, promotion, innovations and other steps for inducing demand.

Such recovery is intricately linked to restructuring the civil aviation sector—having nagging problems at best of times, but now completely grounded. In civil aviation as in tourism, innovations and use of IT for increasing efficiency and productivity and reducing cost should the game changing initiative. Falling aviation fuel cost is a welcome news. The sector will keenly look forward to some cheerful news on ground handling costs.

Even in the best of times the industry had a long wish list. It will now be only longer and more pressing. Government have the huge problem of balancing between falling revenue and need for increasing expenditure — some for reviving the economy much more for social security of the poor and for health safety. It will be pragmatic to stagger the tourism revival plan in a time frame — immediate for survival, short term for recovery and long term for a new journey. And the national economic recovery plan which is likely to create government investments in infrastructure to provide income to the poor should include infrastructure development of domestic tourism destination — the sector that is likely to lead India's tourism resurgence.

Such is the urgency of starting the process of revival of tourism for the economic health of the country that the words of Albert Camus should be a constant reminder "I'll tell you a big secret my friend. Don't wait for the Day of Judgment. It takes place every day."

2

TOURISM DURING AND AFTER COVID-19 — A WORLD VIEW[2]

Travel, John Naisbitt had joyously stated in his book "Global Paradox" in 1994, has made the world a global village. Three decades on, as travel and tourism come to a standstill that village is quiet. International tourism, UNWTO stated, has gone back thirty years. At stake is $1.3 trillion of tourism earnings, global GDP loss of $2 trillion and 100-120 million direct jobs.

Spurred by vast advances in aviation technology, for 40 years of the last century tourism had grown at a rate higher than the growth of the world economy, to become one of the biggest industries. And then at the very beginning of the new millennium the very symbol of tourism—aircraft — was used as the vehicle of doom in 9/11 and tourism growth was dented for the first time. Disasters followed in quick succession—SARS, Tsunami, Financial Crisis. But each time tourism bounced back, so much so that international tourist arrival reached 1.4 billion in 2018, two years ahead of forecast.

Two important lessons were learnt from the experience of the decade of turbulence—lessons that are valid now also. First, travel is in the DNA of human beings and tourism will again bounce back. Second, when international tourism was halted, domestic and regional tourism sustained tourism.

---

2. Engage, HAI, Vol. 1, Issue 3, May-June 2021.

As the enormity of the unprecedented catastrophe slowly sunk in, even in the early stages, many countries responded with relief measures for the tourism and hospitality sector. These measures can be broadly put into four categories.

First, postponement of dues, such as taxes, rents or insurance payments. Egypt, Bulgaria, Italy, Mauritius were among the first to announce such measures. In Malaysia, Tourism tax and service tax are exempted for hotels and entertainment tax for theme parks until 31 Dec 2021. There is a concession of 10-15 percent in electricity dues payable.

Second, Direct aid to companies primarily as pay-roll support. Serbia, Slovenia and Slovakia and Jamaica announced direct payments to companies (or a percentage of salaries) forced to close due to the pandemic. Montenegro provided grants for salaries. Namibia announced a wage subsidy to aid businesses in retaining jobs. Japan provides 75 to 100 percent of daily salary with limit of JPY 15,000 per day as cap. Malaysia provides RM 600 per employee as wage subsidy.

Third, Liquidity issues. Egypt offered tourism facilities low-interest funds and relaxed repayment facilities. Lebanon allowed economic institutions to lend money without interest for five years to help them pay salaries.

Fourth, assistance to workers. Flexibility in terms of social security contributions was implemented by, among others, Greece, Argentina, Kuwait, Morocco, Mongolia, Samoa. In Hungary, state took over 70 percent of lost wages. Gabon, Botswana and South Korea gave employees, placed on technical unemployment an allowance between 50 to 70 percent of their gross salary. Cambodia provided retraining and upskilling programmes and 20 percent of the minimum wages for laid-off workers. Japan provides 80 percent of daily salary with a limit of JPY 11,000 per day as cap.

In India, stunned by the devastating impact of the lockdown measures on the economy, government came out with macro-economic measures to revive the economy. The benefit of some of these measures were expected to percolate down to the hospitality sector as well. But the hospitality sector faces some specific problems and they need specific solutions. Hotel Association of India (HAI)—the industry mouthpiece, has been persistently bringing to the notice of the government the nature of relief needed and they are similar to the broad four categories of global problems mentioned above. There is need for attention to the liquidity problems—review of the interest rates, moratorium and restructuring of loans. Credit is the basic requirement of sound business and the ROR depends on the cost of credit. When the revenue return is almost zero, due to circumstances beyond the control of the industry, it becomes incumbent on the government to review the policy.

The recently announced ECLGS seeks to address some of the problems of the industry but as HAI has pointed out to the FM, many of the well-intended measures are far removed from the ground realities and in effect full benefits do not flow to the intended beneficiaries. The industry is expectantly waiting for positive decision on its dues under the SEIS. HAI's constant advocacy and contact has resulted in some positive response from some state governments like Maharashtra, Punjab and Karnataka on benefits of "industry" status, deferment/waiver of taxes and dues for the period of lockdown.

The Pandemic is shrouded in uncertainty. It has continued longer than originally thought, the second wave has come with greater ferocity and the fear of a third wave is in the air. The industry, particularly the SMEs are struggling to stay alive. Reportedly about 20 percent have gone under.

The most optimistic assessment of UNWTO experts is that international tourism will come back to normal in 2023. Rightly, government have focussed on domestic tourism to push recovery. But the primary facilitators of tourism, the travel agents, the tour operators, the hospitality industry and all other tourism service providers are shattered. Unfortunately, the total impact is not yet known. It is essential that to enable government to frame its policy on firm data, an assessment, even if tentative of the damage should be undertaken.

Some relief measures here and there, and some in some states, have trickled in. It is in the interest of the country, considering the crucial role played by tourism in inclusive growth, considering its multiplier effect in creating jobs, income and demand leading to economic growth, that a plan for relief and revival of tourism is drawn up without delay. It should be comprehensive; it should be national, and it should be built on pragmatic PPP that provides for a systemic, continuous participatory consultation with the private sector.

When tourism comes back, it would have changed considerably. As the recent G-20 discussions and the Punta Cana Declaration of the tourism nations have pointed out, "trust" would be the new currency in travel and sustainability will no longer be an option, it will be a necessity.

Chasing a Ray of Hope

3

A POST COVID RENAISSANCE FOR HOSPITALITY[3]

To say that the coronavirus pandemic has dealt a crippling blow to the Indian travel and tourism industry would be putting it mildly.

The challenges of the previous year had a devastating impact on millions of businesses across the world and the hospitality sector has suffered the most. The overall economic activities have slowly started picking up pace and the gradual removal of travel related restrictions has, spurred optimism for the beleaguered hospitality industry which is limping back to normalcy on the back of domestic leisure business since the last quarter of 2020.

To say that the coronavirus pandemic has dealt a crippling blow to the Indian travel and tourism industry would be putting It mildly. This is a global health crisis that has resulted in the worst recession since World War II and continues to ravage tourism economies the world over - across all levels-national/regional and international and across all market segments - inbound, outbound, domestic, business travel and Events related tourism. The entire Travel & Tourism sector is estimated to lose around US$ 65.57 billion overall. The organised sector alone is likely to lose US$ 25 billion globally. The figures are

3. ET Hospitality World, Feb 23, 2021.

very alarming, and the industry is in dire need of support from all quarters for survival.

Hospitality is capital intensive, people centric industry with very high operating costs as well. What makes it worse is the fact that the costs are largely fixed in nature and allow little scope for cost cutting or cost management. The Industry is battling on many fronts on account of low revenues and disproportionately high costs. It is cash strapped and liquidity is a huge challenge. Hotels are additionally burdened with Increased costs of sanitisation, social distancing and other pandemic related Standard Operating Procedures (SOPs). The recovery is expected to be long and may take 2 to 3 years. For many SMEs this state is not sustainable, and they are on the brink of permanent closure.

Relaxations on inter-state movement have created some travel bubbles. People have been cooped up in their homes for far too long and are traveling to meet friends and relatives and for intimate weddings and get togethers. City dwellers are checking into hotels and resorts located at motorable distances or taking staycations. Green tourism shoots have sprouted in the States of Goa, Uttarakhand, Rajasthan and other locations in the country. The hotels located in these places are poised to experience a high percentage of their pre-covid levels of occupancy though may be not in the Average Daily Revenue. (ADRs). The concerns of health and hygiene have altered consumer behaviour and people are moving to trusted brands offering socially distanced sanitised venues for weddings. With the commencement of the vaccination drive in India, the consumer confidence will grow further. The Industry is hoping for a 20-30 percent increase from the current recovery rate in the coming months. With this, the hospitality sector is set to go into a renaissance in the coming years to ensure hygiene and safety for guests, sustain jobs, and strategize the path to revival by adapting, evolving and innovating to survive in an altered ecosystem.

Against this background 2021 calls for a completely different approach to policy formulation and implementation. One-fourth of the total room inventories will struggle to survive if the industry is not provided support from the government. India has a huge domestic market that can help in an early bounce back as has been seen in the past. Indian tourism can grow at a faster pace than global tourism if supported by pragmatic taxation policies and stimulus packages where the benefits to the economy in the long run far outweigh the costs. The potential of tourism in its contribution to GDP and jobs has already been established. This is to be kept in mind and domestic tourism at all levels has to be incentivised. LTC for the private sector, tax breaks for companies for holding events/conferences within the country are the need of the hour till international and business travel opens up.

The hotels need support to stay afloat and be ready to receive the flood of visitors that is likely to be unleashed as people start to travel when the vaccination drive picks up. Hotels need support in terms of debt restructuring, financing at soft interest rates for working capital needs, rationalisation of taxes, reduced burdens of licence and excise fee, subsidised costs of utilities and much more. For the travel and hospitality sector, 2021 looks to be the year of renaissance, and the industry will darn a new avatar to operate in a world that has been permanently altered by the pandemic. The industry will have to cater to changed consumer behaviour as millennials will travel more than the baby boomers and will have different requirements and demands.

Considering the importance of gearing up for the future the industry was looking to the budget with great hope. Various industry bodies have, while appreciating the economic recovery impetus in the budget have expressed disappointment that the tourism and hospitality sector did not receive the attention it expected and deserved. However, irrespective of omission from the budget the hospitality sector fervently hopes that the clearly demonstrated role of the sector as a catalyst for national economic growth will be acknowledged and all the much-needed impetus will be introduced by the government in the coming days.

4

PREPARING FOR TOURISM AFTER COVID-19

Tourism, it used to be said, made the world a global village. Covid-19 is tearing that village apart.

Ever since World Tourism Organisation (WTO)-- now UNWTO, started keeping record of tourist arrivals globally half a century back, tourism has grown steadily, always outpacing the growth of the world economy. In the process travel and tourism became one of the largest industries in the world creating one in every ten jobs worldwide (330 million) and contributing almost 10 percent of global GDP. In some small island countries, it contributes more than 50 percent of the GDP.

All that now lies shattered with the impact of the vicious spread of Covid-19 that has brought the world to a standstill. UNWTO estimates that in the immediate future tourism growth could be down by 20-30 percent and loss to the industry could be of $30-50 bn. UNWTO hastens to add that due to volatile and uncertain evolution of the pandemic these estimates may need constant review.

At best these estimates could only be rough guesswork and likely to be gross under estimation. World Travel and Tourism Council had pointed out that only about 5 activities that make tourism like accommodation, transport are normally visible and accounted for. But that is only the tip of an iceberg. About thirty other activities and service providers closely associated with travel and tourism economy are not visible directly and difficult to account for. The ripple effects of tourism are deep and wide and if an ironical analogy is permissible, like the spread of Covid-19.

In the first decade of the present century tourism had suffered multiple shocks--from 9/11, the unknown virus again—SARS and the financial crisis. But tourism has always bounced back. There is a difference however in the present crisis. Never before almost the entire globe was locked down totally, never before all modes of transport were so grounded. In earlier crisis domestic tourism and regional tourism sustained the industry. With about 90 percent of the countries of the world sealing the borders as a state policy travel and tourism has been truly halted.

In India too, it may be too early to make a guess about the possible impact. A McKinsey report in circulation shows that of the main sectors of the economy, Airlines and Hotels together are likely to suffer the highest compression of 70-75 percent. Airlines and hotels are only a fragment of the total travel and tourism economy and therefore the enormity of the impact can be easily imagined.

Following the Prime Minister call for "Jan Bhi Jahan Bhi" various economic recovery packages have already been unrolled. Slowly lockdown is expected to be eased and once Covid-19 is reasonably controlled economic activities should pick up fast. But like Charles Handy had said thirty years back *"we are entering an Age of Unreason, ...a time when the only prediction that will hold true is that no predictions will hold true"*. Yet, it is reasonable to presume that return to normalcy will be even slower for the travel and tourism sector. Fear of eruption through contact will take time to go away and tourism demand is likely to be slow in picking up. Nevertheless, lockdown is the correct time to think, to plan and to prepare for the future.

UNWTO has outlined the broad contours of the global response to the crisis—people first and responsible tourism where the tourism response is proportionate to the public health threat but measured to minimize unnecessary interference. The most important need of the hour is to ensure that the tourism support plan is made a part of the national recovery plan. The entire recovery plan should be a joint effort between the central and state governments and the industry. If ever there was a dire need for public private partnership, it is now.

Quite often tourism loses out of the broad picture because of two reasons. First as mentioned above, travel and tourism economy is too diverse and only a few prominent sectors get attention. Secondly, too many diverse sectors within the industry put up too many issues separately and a focused attention on the basics gets lost. It is essential therefore that the industry and the tourism ministry together chalk out a comprehensive and holistic support and promotion plan and ensure that the plan gets due consideration in the national strategy. Globally and in India too, almost 80 percent of the travel and tourism industry is composed of small and medium enterprise. It is the most vulnerable section and as time passes the ability to get on foot for most of them will be further weakened. In most of the countries around the world 'payroll support' and ' liquidity and credit guarantee' are in the front of considerations in this sector and India should be no exception.

Tourism industry would need a lot of incentives to get back in motion from such a crippling shock. There is a demand for providing the status and benefits of 'industry ' to tourism. It is available in some states but often not implemented on ground. 'Industry' status may ease many problems of liquidity and credit. Similarly in the initial stages of recovery all attention should be given to inducing demand. Cost of travel and accommodation naturally should merit a close review and government should seriously examine the demand of the industry for a rationalisation of GST applicable to the sector notwithstanding the dilemma of considering such concessions at a time of falling revenue. Equally seriously the industry should look at cost cutting innovations and use of IT for increased efficiency. Fortunately, it is a time of fall in international oil prices and therefore an opportune time for review of the aviation fuel cost as well as a close look at the ground handling costs at airports.

Even if the industry can quickly get ready on the supply side, the fear of the virus striking back is likely to inhibit travel for some time. Government's responsibility for 'health safety' and security issues would perhaps lead to stricter scrutiny for visas and that may slow down international tourist arrivals for some time.

And that is the time to prepare for domestic tourism—spruce up the destinations, invest in tourism infrastructure development in a way that income is created in the rural areas. Before Covid-19 India had the tremendous resource of close to 1500 million visits by domestic tourists. That is the force that will be game changer in post-Covid-19 recovery. Very appropriately the tourism recovery plan must start with investments to create world class infrastructure in the "Swadesh Darshan" scheme. Most tourism activities are within the purview of the state governments and therefore each state should prepare a state specific revival plan in association with the private sector in conformity with the national plan. It is also a time for bringing the concept of 'responsible tourism' to the forefront of tourism revival plans. The flagship "PRASHAD" scheme of pilgrim tourism can lead the way providing the much needed opportunity for thanks giving post-Covid-19. And the Buddhist Circuit should be spruced up imaginatively so that when the time is opportune regional tourists can be attracted — and that will be a stepping stone to launch promotion leading to large scale international tourist arrivals.

5

A RAY OF HOPE?[4]

Various government measures that can be taken apart from those mentioned in the Budget 2021 for the revival and growth of tourism.

"Perhaps it is time to collate the lessons of this pandemic and see if some such plan for automatic disaster management response for the sector which also provides insurance and social security umbrella and income and liquidity support to the most vulnerable sections of the industry could be devised."

"All indicators are positive for calibrated reopening of international travel"—this recent statement of the Tourism Secretary must have come as a ray of hope for the beleaguered tourism industry.

When in March 2020 the country had gone into a complete lockdown, bringing tourism to standstill, the gravity of the situation had not yet completely sunk in. There was hope that like the SARS, it will pass. Soon the worries deepened to apprehension and in no time became a trauma of catastrophe. It was much beyond the control of the industry and much beyond what the industry composed of 80-90 percent of SMEs could withstand on its own. Therefore, the industry, largely self-dependent in normal times looked desperately to government for help—for survival.

---

4. BW Hotelier, 01 March 2021.

The demands of the industry were mostly related to micro-management - liquidity support in the short run, deferment of interest payments, statutory fiscal liabilities, GST, utility costs to be charged on actuals, credit guarantee support, waiver of annual licence fee for the period just to mention a few. Some of them were within the competence of the Central government, others with the State governments and all of them were eminently justified and easily doable. In fact, the Minister Tourism in his many interactions with the industry appreciated the importance of resolving these issues and perhaps tried to facilitate. Yet, as the industry is now looking for revival it feels that during this gloomy period nothing much happened by way of relief. Whatever happened were scattered and piecemeal and not uniform for the whole country. The response of the government to the problems of the industry was not fast enough.

Tourism industry was looking to the national economic recovery programmes announced by the government with great hope but again the specific problems of the tourism sector remained unaddressed. Tattered and bruised, the industry or whatever of it that has been able to withstand the storm so far was looking for revival to start and pinned its hope on the budget announcements. The budget has been lauded for its focus on economic development, but tourism and hospitality industry again find itself left in the lurch.

No doubt, as the tourism secretary and many others have pointed out many of the infrastructure development investments will indirectly or directly benefit tourism also. However, such investments have a gestation period and the effects on tourism will be largely indirect. The industry gasping for breath needs immediate succour. Given a will, such relief, ironically is possible. It is heartening, in that context to note that the CEO of Niti Aayog reportedly told the recent ITM that relief measures for tourism and hospitality sector need not necessarily flow from the budget and they can be provided in the normal course of government action. Taking a cue from that tourism industry will be keenly looking forward to some favourable measures to kick start the revival process.

The starting of international travel as mentioned by the tourism secretary will be one step towards the revival process. But, as he has indicated, it will start in a small measure and will be a small push for the time being dependent on many imponderables. The big push and the more immediate one to happen will come, as has been often talked about, from domestic tourism. Revival will be faster if the government, considering the very unprecedented circumstances in which the industry is placed takes proactive measures to facilitate growth of tourism. The biggest casualty of the pandemic has been public confidence. Therefore, measures to boost confidence should be at the top of the agenda. Luckily, the start of vaccination has been a very big step forward though there is much more to be done still.

Government will have to ensure that the SOPs for health and safety are harmonised among the states and among different government agencies responsible for their implementation. Reopening of domestic tourism and tourism related services experienced bottlenecks due to conflicting SOPs of different states.

Secondly, a pragmatic PPP initiative will have to be evolved to ensure that all the service providers like the hotels, restaurants, the transport providers, tour operators, travel agents and others are in sync to create that atmosphere of confidence. Third, in the initial stages the PPP measures should include practical incentives both for travellers and the service providers for safe travel. Foreign exchange incentive schemes like SIES should be remodelled and introduced. Fourth, the much-needed relief for the tourism industry should be provided without further delay so that the service providers can be on their feet to make tourism happen.

The disaster that happened in the form of COVID-19 can happen again, maybe not in the same scale or intensity. The experience of past year has shown that while the disaster management protocol takes care of the health, safety, relief and rescue needs, the specific economic survival problems of tourism industry must be handled by a specific sector strategy. Perhaps it is time to collate the lessons of this pandemic and see if some such plan for automatic disaster management response for the sector which also provides insurance and social security umbrella and income and liquidity support to the most vulnerable sections of the industry could be devised.

We have been aware of the impact of the pandemic on thousands of hotels, restaurants, tour operators, transport providers and the picture is grim. We have not yet realised the impact on millions who indirectly depend on tourism and hospitality for their livelihood. It is said that of the thirty odd core activities that make tourism only five or six are visible. The ripple effects throughout the economy are often not captured in statistics. As a result, the policymakers do not fully realise the economic significance of tourism. It is reported that the Ministry of Tourism is trying to assess the full impact of the pandemic on total employment and livelihood in tourism related activities. Such an exercise is very urgently needed to establish the importance of the sector in the national economy enabling it to get the recognition it deserves.

6

HOSPITALITY BRACES FOR A SURGE IN DEMAND[5]

The ecosystem is marked by a sense of confidence for the future, reflected in visible action all around to make "atmanirbhar" a reality.

There is excitement in the air in the hospitality sector about an unprecedented surge in demand. Tourism has seen a strong rebound since the festive season in 2022, buoyed by domestic tourism as well as by gradual pick up of international tourist arrivals. The pent-up demand was expected and is now further fuelled by new found enthusiasm in the economy and revival of consumer demand.

There are plenty of reports from the ground to substantiate the authenticity of this surge. They also indicate that the hospitality ecosystem is changing, marked by robust response to emerging challenges of technology adoption, and of meeting the demands of customers empowered by technology for servicing experiences. The ecosystem is marked by a sense of confidence for the future, reflected in visible action all around to make "atmanirbhar" a reality.

The hospitality industry witnessed a strong Q3 FY23 with improved RevPAR (Revenue Per Available Room) and an increase in

5. ET Hospitality World, May 24, 2023.

the ARR (Average Room Rate). As per a report by Motilal Oswal, the occupancy rate (OR) stood at 65 percent in Q3 FY23, just slightly lower than pre-covid-19 levels. Industry assessments indicate that OR will surpass pre- covid levels in the coming quarters driven by some major tailwinds such as the wedding season, G-20 Summit meetings, the ICC ODI Cricket World Cup and revival of foreign inbound travel. All tourism levers, such as MICE, inbound traffic, med tourism, business and leisure travel are on the rise. Care Edge estimates that RevPAR should grow 3-5 percent over FY23 levels.

Many other reports and surveys confirm the upward swing in demand. As per MakeMyTrip, the average number of room nights per booking for the ongoing April-June quarter has increased for both domestic and outbound holiday packages. Estimates from travel agents and tour operators suggest that summer vacation bookings are up by 30 percent this year for domestic and international travel. The business travel and entertainment (T&E) survey report titled 'Revival of business travel: An India perspective' commissioned by American Express, India with the Centre for Economics and Business Research (CEBR), shows that majority of Indian businesses (67 percent) expect a rise in business travel in 2023 and 77 percent of business houses are expecting to increase their travel budget in 2023 as compared to 2022.

These are unmistakable signs of its resurgence for Indian hospitality as compared to situation during the pandemic when the very survival of the Sector was at stake. It is well known that the World Travel & Tourism Council (WTTC) ranks India as 10th largest travel and tourism economy globally. The Ministry of Tourism has a vision to make India one of the top five destinations with a trillion-dollar tourism economy. The positive business sentiment has coincided with some important policy announcements by the government. In addition to campaigns like Dekho Apna Desh, schemes like Swadesh Darshan, e-visas on arrival, the Union Budget of 2023-24 has called for promotion of tourism in a mission mode with active participation of states, convergence of government programmes and public-private partnerships.

Hospitality industry is at the centre of this new vision. It has a key role to play in satisfying the primary reason for travel - a good experience. And the vision cannot become a reality without the needed expansion of quality accommodation. A survey by HVS Anarock brings out a number of interesting statistics.

Hotel companies accelerated their growth plans in 2022 because of the strong recovery in demand, which led to a 33 percent year-over-year increase in brand signings by keys 166 new hotels with 14,885 rooms were added to the branded hotel market in 2022, while 90 hotels with 5,702 rooms underwent rebranding. The study says the average room count is declining as hotel operators enter smaller markets. Domestic hotel operators continued to sign more properties (75 percent of the total signings by property) than their international counterparts, with an average key count of 68 keys in 2022. Tier 3 & 4 tier cities accounted for 47 percent of the total signings by property in 2022. Midscale hotels remain the market leader for hotels signed in 2022 with 48 percent signed properties. Still there is a long way to go. Reportedly as on 31 December 2022, India had a little over 28,000 branded rooms in the leisure segment spread across the entire country - minuscule compared even with nearby Bali and Phuket having around 1,20,000 branded rooms.

For years the hospitality industry has been pleading with the government to make two fundamental changes to facilitate the industry to help in much needed expansion of accommodation and infrastructure-grant of infrastructure status and industry status. Fresh wind is now blowing in the tourism sector. There is much talk of development in mission mode, and strong PPP. But inexplicably the basic demands of the industry have eluded attention. Undeterred, the hospitality industry has shown great resilience and heartening response to the market demands and commitments to the national goals by taking up expansion plans. These expansion plans go beyond the metros and cover all categories of hotels.

There is much news to cheer. One headline states- Investments in the Indian hospitality sector are likely to exceed US$ 2.3 billion (about INR 19,000 crore) over the next two to five years, according to the first-ever hospitality report released by real estate consulting firm CBRE South Asia. The report titled 'Hospitality Sector. On a Comeback Trail, said that the total investment during 2020-2023 is likely to exceed US$ 0.4 billion (about INR 3,295 crore)."

7

AWAITING A NEW VOICE[6]

Though the industry in general has revived largely, there are finer points of this revival which merit close attention. There is need to worry more about revenue rather than numbers.

"For last year's words belong to last year's language. And next year's words await another voice." —TS Eliot

Philosophically the New Year is just another day, an artificial landmark in the march of the time juggernaut. Psychologically it is a new beginning, a new hope, a time to look forward and leave the failings of the times past in the past.

Tourism and Hospitality industries eagerly look forward to the new year for a new beginning. The scars of the traumatic years left behind have not yet healed fully. The year 2022 certainly brought a lot of cheer and much confidence. But everyone realises that there are bigger challenges ahead and it is the time to lay the foundation for a strong, secure future.

Tourism and Hospitality industries therefore hope that the much-discussed new Tourism Policy will herald the new year. It can certainly be said that a policy is merely a statement of intent and often is left in the wayside unless committed implementation follows. Nevertheless, a policy is significant because it lays down the future directions of the journey, and all that makes the journey meaningful and successful.

---

6. Engage, HAI, Vol 2, Issue 6, Nov—Dec. 2022.

There is much urgency because the draft policy has much to commend itself and many of the intended actions brook no delay. It is also meaningful that the draft coincided with the formulation of a new vision for a new India @47. The Ministry of Tourism had wide-ranging discussions with all the stakeholders and all conceivable issues, ideas, suggestions came up. Fortunately, the Draft Policy covers all the wish list of the industry. It talks of tourism as a global opportunity for India. It emphatically says that "national priority is a must" for tourism—something that HAI has persistently been urging. Rightly, it recommends a holistic framework for tourism development—of various government departments, of central and state governments, of people and the private sector. It is a desirable framework but a difficult one to achieve and needs all the attention of the government to do so. The Draft Policy is built around five key guiding principles, five national missions and ten strategic-pillars covering all that the industry had ventilated—digital reach, sustainable goals, skill development, professional destination management and so on.

It is understandable that the future vision has been expressed mostly in terms of impressive growth statistics—reflecting the demand side, like one trillion-dollar tourism economy, 100 m FTAs, 2.3 bn domestic tourism visits, $ 250 in foreign exchange earnings, 100 m direct employment. In the enthusiasm often two key parameters get blurred. First, the need to worry more about revenue rather than numbers. The imperative need is to look at the supply side—in infrastructure (transport, communication and all that), the trained technology savvy service providers creating an experience rather than a visit, and above all sustainable development of destinations and quality accommodation. The mismatch between the quantitative aspirations often expressed by the government and the realities on the supply side like air seat capacity, accommodation, carrying capacity of known destinations, have not properly been addressed yet. Unless that is done carefully the vision may remain an unrealistic wish list.

In that context, the persistent pleading of HAI before the government to give "infrastructure status" to hospitality industry is based on impeccable logic and sound common sense. The logic extends the concept of "Atmanirbhar" and in essence says – enable and empower the industry to come up with much needed investments to fill the gap in accommodation. There will be no dent on government revenue and in fact the long-term return to the exchequer will be enormous.

It also defies all logic and understanding as to why tourism and hospitality, the biggest industry in the world, the biggest employment generator, the best contributor to inclusive growth be not encouraged to grow manifold and contribute to national welfare by allowing to enjoy the benefits that the government extends to an organised industry. Everyone agrees—the Ministry of Tourism, the Parliamentary Standing Committee and all, and the PM calls it a pillar of development. Yet the industry languishes, and a decision eludes. It is to be hoped that in the new year, someone will bell the cat.

Of greatest interest to the industry is the restatement in the draft policy of the fundamental principle of tourism promotion—a private sector-led growth. It has often remained a slogan. The Tourism and Hospitality sector is enthused by the concept of National Tourism Authority and State Tourism Authority. Of more interest was a subsequent statement from the MOT that a National Tourism Board was being set up. It will be a fitting implementation of the intention to lead tourism promotion through the private sector. This was one of the key recommendations of the National Tourism Committee of 1987 and if properly constituted will bring in the type of professional tourism management that say Singapore Tourism Board signifies.

Though the industry in general has revived largely, there are finer points of this revival which merit close attention. Globally, as in India, tourism and hospitality sectors comprise almost 80 percent of SMEs. This sector was badly mauled by the pandemic and its after-effects. Imaginative and constructive liquidity solutions are crucial to the full recovery and growth of this sector. HAI had advocated a long term transparent and stable interest rate policy during the period of survival. There have been some ad hoc and sporadic responses to overcome immediate problems. The industry would look forward to a comprehensive and pragmatic policy package on the liquidity problems of the industry.

The Covid-19 pandemic was a great shock, a jolt difficult to withstand and overall, a great lesson on survival. HAI had advocated at that time that innovative and imaginative public private partnership initiatives should be launched to protect the vulnerable from future shocks and unexpected disruption of business. It is possible to create a participatory future fund in the pattern of a social security umbrella.

Rightly, the new year starts with cautious optimism, because as is often said, the only thing that can be said about the future is that nothing can be said with certainty. For the Indian tourism and hospitality industry, it should be a time for reflection and for preparing for the journey armed with the lessons learnt. One unmistakable lesson, put in the words of UNWTO, is that Covid-19 "is a watershed moment to align the effort of sustaining livelihoods dependent on tourism to SDG and ensure a more resilient, inclusive, carbon neutral and resource-efficient future". The trend is unmistakable—towards taking cognizance of environmental costs beyond economic costs; destinations moving towards a zero-carbon footprint; tour operators and hoteliers gravitating towards more responsible and meaningful experiences.; showcasing local for global; and positioning the host community as the centrepiece of the tourist experience, and technology ruling the roost.

UNWTO recently advocated rethinking of tourism. In an unprecedented discussion the UN General Assembly urged the nations to rebuild tourism for the planet and for the people. The tourism and hospitality industry is waiting for that "new language" and the "new voice" in the NEW YEAR.

8

RING OUT THE OLD, RING IN THE NEW[7]

The industry has faced yet another year of struggle, battling misconceptions, unforeseen circumstances and different pandemic waves. Embracing automation, pivoting to sustainable practices and vast skilling/reskilling will help to rebuild faster.

"For last year's words belong to last year's language and next year's words await another voice." – TS Eliot.

The hospitality industry so much looks forward to a new experience – another voice – in the year 2022 after the harrowing travails of a year that is best forgotten! The last year was a year of hope and of frustrations. In the initial stages the industry was looking at signs of revival, but soon as the prolonged pandemic and resultant close downs hit the industry, "survival" again became the predominant concern.

The year was not only of struggle but also of realisation of some hard truths. The first was that tourism and hospitality, the sunrise industry, a pillar of development employing 10 percent of the total employment directly and millions indirectly, providing 8 percent of GDP, must fend for itself when the chips are down. The industry

7. Engage, Vol. 2, Issue 1, Jan-Feb 2022.

encountered rude misconception that it is elitist whereas 80 percent of the industry is composed of MSEs, and this highly capital-intensive sector is exposed to payment of statutory liabilities and revenue expenditure even when the government-imposed restrictions brought income to near zero.

HAI was constantly engaged in a continuing series of activities to create public awareness about the distress of the vital sector, to strengthen advocacy with the government at different levels, to seek meaningful relief and to forge collaboration with other industry organisations to create a single voice for the industry.

It soon dawned that policy making in the government is diffused. The Ministry of Tourism was sensitive to the problems of the industry and their solutions, but it was only a catalyst and the power of redressal lay elsewhere – RBI, Ministry of Finance, Ministry of Commerce etc. The macroeconomic relief packages passed the sector by. Whatever little came mostly to address the problem of liquidity faced the question of implementation. The banks had their own compulsions and the fine prints stood on the way of substantive relief flowing to the needy. The states had the power to give some relief from statutory dues etc., but there was no single point of approach, each state had its own way of response. Some states did respond, though late but most did not. Again, the greatest hurdle to recovery was the multiplicity of covid protocols and their complexity, lack of cohesion between states and lack of coordination. The pandemic may peter out soon, but the flaws in the system that the experience of the year exposed should not be lost sight of while planning for future preparedness.

The year exposed the utter helplessness of the substantial and most vulnerable sector of the industry – the MSMEs. There was no visible policy for their relief. How many went under, how many forever, are not yet known. UNWTO has provided some global figures. The contribution of tourism to the global economy amounted to US$3.5 trillion in 2019 i.e. 4 percent of world GDP and it reduced by US$ 2 trillion in 2020 which is about 70 percent of the overall decline in world GDP in 2020. International tourist arrivals dropped by 73 percent and by the end of 2021 still remained 72 percent below the previous level.

Early 2021 there were hopeful signs and the industry edged up slowly. But the bad news is that tourism is not expected to return to the pre-pandemic level until 2024 at the earliest. This year therefore will see struggle for survival to continue while laying the foundation for revival should engage greater attention.

Miserable as the year has been, 2021 is looked upon as an experience to build the future. And there is plenty to draw upon.

Various studies and surveys during this year have shown that the hospitality world has changed and that the changes are not likely to be transient. There are indications that tourism demand will surge in 2022. A reported Google study for US consumers revealed that 56 percent of those surveyed were likely to travel in the next two years. Significantly those surveyed spent 71 percent of their time researching online. Most travellers value previous experiences with the selected brand and price is a major factor as is the flexibility in booking and cancellations. A dominant deciding factor is the response of the brands to safety, health and environmental concerns. A reported study of Indian travellers done by Thomas Cook and SOTC also points to similar findings – 66 percent of those surveyed said that they were willing to pay extra for trust – in health and safety standards. Thus, "confidence" and brand reputation are emerging as increasingly important factors in consumer choices.

There is almost unanimous agreement that digital transformation will be the most visible and enduring change to affect the industry. During the peak of the pandemic, it was used primarily for reducing physical interaction. But digitalisation will no longer be a short-term fix to overcome the pandemic problems. It has become a tool for cutting-edge advantage in price war and shift in business strategies. A global survey by McKinsey of 800 senior executives in 2020 showed that two-thirds of them had stepped up investments in automation. The digital experience is however going much beyond automation.

For example, (a) the hotels can use digital technology to access data for proactive personalised marketing. (b) It can make the new trend of staycation a reliable, innovative and enjoyable reality. (c) It can help in easy access to consumer data base and its centralisation. In fact, an Amadeus study affirms that increasing digitalisation need not be in conflict with increasing personalisation – which is the strength of hospitality business. With wider access to and use of expanding data base at its disposal combined with integrated technology, hotels can make customer experiences very personal and unique. (d) Digitalisation is likely to be used more and more for shift from revenue management to profit management by allowing access to shared data across business "not just in silos". The strategic use of wider range of data and integrated technology are expected to lead to proactive decision making, increase efficiency in operation and reduce operational cost.

The world has moved fast to grab the new opportunities that use of technology offers to bring tourism back on rail. UNWTO mentions that already 12000 startups in 160 countries are working with 300 corporate partners on new tourism technologies suitable to the post-pandemic realities. India is the world leader in information technology. Here is an opportunity for the hospitality sector to get together to initiate a tourism technology revolution. At the same time both government and industry together have a very urgent role of skilling the existing and new entrants in the new requirements.

Attention to skilling is assuming importance because of another phenomenon noticed in USA, Australia, New Zealand and some European countries. Globally tourism employment is expected to rise by 18 percent in 2022, still 10 m jobs less than the 2019 level. However, these countries have faced very serious labour shortages as recovery is in the upswing. The nature of job losses in tourism and hospitality sector is presumed to be very heavy in India but a clear picture is not yet available. In the context of high unemployment, the industry is unlikely to face labour shortages but once the industry is on the growth path redistribution of skilled personnel lost during the pandemic may be a reality. Rapid tourism development targeted by the country would lead to expansion of hospitality infrastructure and resultant growth in employment. Getting personnel skilled in the new demand for technology-oriented skills should be on top of the agenda for action.

"It is imperative that we rebuild the tourism sector in a safe, equitable and climate friendly manner," UN Secretary-General Antonio Guterres has said – here "we" is the key to such rebuilding.

9

TOURISM AND HOSPITALITY—PARTNERSHIP FOR REVIVAL[8]

" .....be still and wait without hope, for hope would be hope for the wrong thing;"

Perhaps this quote from T.S.Eliot is an apt description of the state in which the tourism and hospitality sector in India is—devastated by the pandemic and torn now between hope and disillusionment.

Still the industry dares to hope. What inspires this optimism? First, the massive vaccination programme bringing back the most important factor for revival—confidence—and a hope that the worst is behind us. The tourism secretary recently said as much. "All indicators are positive for calibrated reopening of international travel"—he said in relation to opening of international tourism. He was naturally cautious. It has to be gradual depending on the situation. With most of the source markets –USA, UK and Europe reeling under the new strands of virus, the opening up has to be carefully calibrated. The hope for tourism revival depends therefore on domestic tourism and short haul markets and regional tourism, perhaps to the east. To boost domestic tourism, government can, apart from many other things, help to make travel easier and cheaper. Air travel can be cheaper if aviation fuel costs, local taxes and ground handling costs are carefully

8. Engage, Vol. 1, Issue 2, Mar-April 2021.

examined and rationalised. Even the airlines which are under stress will welcome any such pragmatic move to cut costs where possible. There should be incentives to prop up the demand side. LTC is only a fringe and the idea has to be fine tuned to make it beneficial to the tourism industry. Lowering of GST in hotels and restaurants even if temporarily will be a big step for revival. The cost-benefit analysis of such a revision may show that the gain to GDP may far outweigh the visible loss in revenue on the GST account.

Globally it is recognised that tourism and hospitality is one of the worst hit sectors. To provide relief to the beleaguered industry, considering its employment and income generating dimensions, many countries have come up with measures like payroll support, liquidity and credit guarantee for the MSME/SME sector lending. Even in the early stages of the pandemic when the devastation was looming large, one Niti Aayog presentation had also identified these as possible stimulus measures to consider for the Indian economy. At policy level, the tourism industry and HAI have steadfastly brought these to the attention of the policy makers.

Government's big economic recovery programmes unfortunately did not have anything directly for tourism industry. May be some of the investment benefits would trickle down to benefit the tourism sector. But that is at best a distant possibility. Therefore, the industry was eagerly looking forward to the budget for some immediate succor. Alas, there was none. None of the policy measures identified by Niti Aayog, nor the ground level measures pointed out by the industry were addressed. The consolation offered is –many of the infrastructure sector investments will indirectly benefit tourism also. Again, that is only a possibility and in the long run. Tourism and hospitality industry striving for revival can only ruefully remember the famous saying of economist Keynes- "in the long run we are all dead".

Still the industry latches on to HOPE—that irrespective of the budget, government can and will do something in the normal course of governance to mitigate some of the grievances soon. It can extend the benefits of industry to the tourism sector. Some states like Maharashtra, Karnataka, Telangana, Punjab have shown the way and government can make it uniform for the country. The benefits of social infrastructure provided earlier is now on hold. Government can renew this incentive, remove the time limit and increase the capital investment limit to Rs 200 crore to make visible dent in social infrastructure sector. Third, the incentives under SEIS, which are earned by the industry should be restored. Fourth, some of the very legitimate demands like deferment of statutory payments, licence fees, GST deferment etc should be accepted. These are small steps for the government but are giant strides for the industry at this time of stress. Lastly it is necessary to harmonise all the health and safety SOPs across the country for hassle free growth of tourism.

The industry too will have to introspect and collaborate with the government on all the health and safety measures and put them in place effectively. It must bring in effective confidence building measures. It should focus on innovative measures to reduce costs for boosting demand.

If there ever was a dire need for meaningful partnership it is NOW.

10

STEPPING OUT AGAIN

Travel and tourism have been one of the world's largest industries, creating one in every 10 jobs (330 million) globally, and contributing almost 10 of global GDP. All that now lies shattered after the Covid-19 pandemic.

The UN World Tourism Organisation estimates that in the immediate future, tourism growth could be down by 20-30 percent, and loss to the industry could be down by 20-30 percent, and loss to the industry could be $30-50 billion. These estimates are likely to be underestimation.

About 30 other activities and service providers closely associated with the travel and tourism economy are difficult to account for. The ripple effects of tourism in shambles are deep and wide.

A McKinsey report shows that airlines and hotels together (making only a fragment of the tourism economy) are likely to suffer the highest compression among sectors — of 70-75 percent. One can reasonably presume that return to normalcy will be slower for the travel and tourism sector than others.

It is essential that the tourism support plan is made part of the national recovery one and is a joint effort between the central and state governments, and the industry. If ever there was a dire need for public-private partnership (PPP), it is now.

Globally, including in India, almost 80 percent of the travel and tourism industry is composed of small and medium enterprises (SMEs). In most countries, 'payroll support' and 'liquidity and credit guarantee' are priority considerations in this sector. India should be no exception. 'Industry' status to the sector is available in some states, but it's often not implemented on the ground.

Providing industry status may ease many problems of liquidity and credit. Cost of travel and accommodation should merit a close review and government should seriously examine the demand for rationalisation of goods and services tax (GST) applicable to the sector, notwithstanding the dilemma of considering such concessions at a time of falling revenue.

The industry should also look at cost-cutting innovations and use IT for increased efficiency. Fortunately, with international oil prices having fallen, this is an opportune time for the cost of aviation fuel to be reviewed and, in conjunction, ground-handling costs at airports.

GoI's responsibility for 'health safety' and security issues should lead to stricter scrutiny for visas, and that may indeed slow down international tourist arrivals for some time. Which is why this could be exactly the time to prepare for domestic tourism — spruce up destinations invest in tourism infrastructure development in a way that income is created in the rural areas, etc.

Before Covid-19, India had close to 1,500 million visits by domestic tourists. That is the force that can be a game-changer in post-Covid-19 recovery. A tourism recovery plan must start with investments to create world-class infrastructure in a 'Swadesh Darshan' scheme. Most tourism activities are within the purview of state governments.

So, each state should prepare a state specific revival plan in association with the private sector in conformity with the national plan. This is also a time to bring the concept of 'responsible tourism' to the forefront of tourism revival plans.

The flagship PRASAD (Pilgrimage Rejuvenation and Spiritual Augmentation Drive) scheme for pilgrim tourism can lead the way. The

'Buddhist circuit', for instance, should be spruced up imaginatively, so that when the time is right, regional tourists can be attracted.

That, in turn, will be a stepping stone for largescale international tourist arrivals.

Learning the Lessons and Picking up the Threads

11

HAS COVID-19 CHANGED TOURISM AND HOSPITALITY? -1[9]

Change happens. Embrace it. Reset growth by focusing on sustainability and touchless services. However, the digital switch must not lose out on unique experiences.

The book Who Moved My Cheese? by Dr Spencer Johnson, which sold 28 million copies, deals with the problem of change and illustrates that those who do not adapt to change perish. It's similar to Darwin's theory—those who adapt survive.

The World Tourism Organisation (UNWTO) looked at the emerging trends during Covid-19 and found that the popular choices now include closer-to-home travel, staycations, rural, nature-oriented, and open air. Health, safety concerns, flexibility in travel arrangements and bookings are key consumer concerns. There Is a change in demographics with more young travellers. Consumers are more concerned about responsible travel, sustainable travel, local eco-systems, and authenticity of experience. Are these trends going to stay? How should the industry respond?

There are myriad ways to respond, to innovate and to think out-of-the-box solutions. Adversity brings new opportunities.

9. Engage, Vol. 1, Issue 4, July-Aug 2021.

A study across 10 countries and 11,000 travellers, done by Edelmen for Travelport, shows that transparency about pricing, health and safety norms, flexibility in bookings and safety of personal data in digital transactions, as some of the major concerns of the consumers. Nearly half of the respondents chose "trust" over all other factors when choosing a travel supplier. This factor explains why hotels have seen more of direct bookings. Consumers have been guided by the brand image and trust in a brand more than anything else.

It is inevitable that there will be a paradigm shift in the relationship with customers, as part of the new management strategy. This shift will be guided by data and technology. As technology is likely to be more openly available to everyone, innovation in using it is likely to provide the cutting edge. A recent study by two travel houses, Thomas Cook and SOTC, has shown that personal health and safety are the top concerns for 70 percent of the respondents, 80 percent preferred friendly and flexible cancellation policies, and 77 percent thought that in these uncertain times, transparent communication, guidance and reassurance from the service providers are essential.

"Trust", it has been rightly said, is the new currency. Information sharing and communication with the consumer are going to be the most important management response requirements. As the pandemic has been unpredictable, and the protocols have been changing often and varying from place to place, the importance of providing up-to-date, authentic information cannot be overstated. It shows the service providers' commitment and responsibility and enhances consumer confidence.

While responding to consumer concerns, digital transformation is the most important management tool. In a survey by Skift, a travel and hospitality media outlet, 78 percent of the travel and hospitality industry executives considered digital transformation more important than before. Digital transformation has its implications both for the supply side as well as the demand side. On the demand side, it facilitates communication and information flow. On the supply side, it will enable contactless experiences—checking-in, checking-out, opening the room, taking care of customer requirements, and improving health and hygiene. The possibilities are endless.

While the primary objective of technology will be to build consumer confidence, it will also bring in a number of side benefits like flexibility in operations, providing agility to respond to market trends, customisation and personalisation, perhaps greater access to consumer data, which can be used, for a stronger relationship, feedback on services, and loyalty initiatives. In the long run, it will increase productivity and reduce costs.

However, a few questions arise, and answer to those will show the quality of imaginative management. Workcations, combining business and leisure is becoming the norm. How to make the connectivity hassle-free? How to provide home ambience for work? Will robots and contactless service take away the most distinguishing factor in hospitality service—personal touch and unique experience?

While the digital switch provides benefits of consumer data and online payment gateways, consumer confidence will be bolstered by assurances of personal data confidentiality, cyber security and protection against fraud.

The pandemic had brought tremendous awareness about sustainability. It has changed attitudes, and widened understanding about the imperatives of a sustainable approach. Tourism and environment have a two-way relationship. A clean environment is essential for tourism growth. Tourism can help in promoting such an environment, or in the reverse, may damage environment. UNWTO has often said that while only three points in Sustainable Development Goals directly mention tourism, tourism has a role to play in almost every goal. While so far, sustainability had been looked upon as a desirable objective, the pandemic has made it a necessity. Customers are more likely now to expect sustainability in behaviour and sensitivity to sustainable norms—reduced use of plastics, efficient energy use and water management, waste management, disaster management, human rights issues—as part of their choice.

It follows therefore that those who are proactive in these matters will have the advantage in the post-Covid competitive world. In a recent report, CII has emphasized this role—"enterprises are intrinsic to the sustainability solution." Airlines are already talking of biofuel and have committed to carbon neutrality by 2050. It has been reported that the global carbon dioxide emissions fell by 6.4 percent—approximately 2.3 billion tons—in 2020 when travel had almost stopped.

Tourism will bounce back, so will demand. Competition for bookings will remain the battleground. Rapid changes are taking place. To quote Who Moved My Cheese? again: "Let go of old cheese quicker so you can find new cheese sooner."

12

HAS THE PANDEMIC CHANGED TOURISM? -2[10]

"The only thing that can be said with certainty about the future is that nothing can be said with certainty. Recovery outlook, according to UNWTO remains cautious. Its panel of experts expect revival to happen only in 2022 at the earliest."

Just when the tourism industry had seen 'a ray of hope' in the beginning of the new year the pandemic has come back with greater fury. Things are, so to say, back to square one. However, even in this unfolding gloom there is optimism - that with the coverage of most of the population with vaccination and with higher herd immunity the pandemic will settle down in a few months and tourism can be revived.

With that optimism it is now time to carefully plan the revival. Will it be business as usual for tourism or have things changed? Certainly, the numbers have changed. So has attitudes and preferences of consumers. While the numbers can be built again, it would be prudent to take note of the changes that are discernible.

As for numbers, COVID-19 has brought tourism to a complete standstill. International tourism is back to the levels of what was 30

---

10. BW Hotelier, 29 April 2021.

years ago. Effects of tourism spread across many activities creating what is called 'ripple effects' throughout the economy. That total impact has not yet been assessed. But UN- WTO (World Tourism Organisation) points out what is at stake - 100-120 mn direct jobs, loss of up to US$ 1.2 trillion in international visitors spending and loss of US $2 trillion of global GDP.

UNWTO has indicated some of the broad changes in trends which are likely to be more established in the future. Health and Safety measures and cancellation policies are consumers' main concerns. From such concerns emerge their primary preferences for sustainability, authenticity and 'localhood'. Travellers are giving more importance to creating a positive impact on local communities, increasingly looking for authenticity. Nature, Rural Tourism and Road Trips have emerged as popular travel choices due to renewed interest in sustainability, travel limitations and the quest for open-air, off the beaten track experiences. Travellers are also aware of their responsibility and expect similar awareness from the host communities. Domestic tourism has shown positive signs in many markets since people tend to travel to closer destinations. Travellers go for 'staycations' or vacations close to home. Because of concern for health and safety travel recovery has been stronger among younger segments. 'Mature' travellers and retirees are likely to be the most impacted segments in the immediate future.

In 2015, when the world adopted the SDG - a 2030 agenda for a transformation world, tourism was mentioned only in Goals 8, 12 and 14 but it was seen that tourism could contribute directly or indirectly to all the goals. It is felt that the pandemic may seriously compromise the achievements of the goals, but it also provides an opportunity to reemphasise the overarching need for sustainability to save the only planet we have. As UNWTO says Covid-19 "is a watershed moment to align the effort of sustaining livelihoods dependent on tourism to SDG and ensure a more resilient, inclusive, carbon neutral and resource efficient future".

No wonder that recently UNWTO made the Tbilishi declaration

affirming commitment to work towards a sustainable recovery of tourism. It defined that future plans and policies should put people first, allowing tourism to restart safely, accelerate economic recovery and provide hope for millions of people.

In India, there is no doubt that the first push for revival of tourism will come from domestic tourism. Even during the brief lull in the pandemic when travel and movement restrictions were eased, the pent-up demand had filled up resorts and destinations near metropolitan cities. India has huge tourism attractions of very wide variety—nature, wildlife, mythology, history, culture, heritage. Even when tourism has been absent, Ministry of Tourism has kept the campaign for domestic tourism – 'Dekho Apna Desh' - in full swing. To make domestic tourism an engine of inclusive growth lot of efforts have to go into creating suitable infrastructure like communication facilities to make travel easy and affordable, accommodation that caters to health and hygiene standards, imaginative wayside facilities and sustainable destination development. If the local community is to benefit economically, local craft, cuisine, culture will have to be integrated to destination development. To create a good experience, authentic and effective story telling is also essential. Trained local guides can fill up this gap. It is heartening to note that the draft Tourism Policy of the government has put professional destination management with the involvement of the local community as a priority area.

Responsible tourism that caters to creating a sustainable experience and safe hygienic destinations is possible when the responsibility is shared by all the stakeholders - government, local community, tourists and service providers in the private sector - in partnership. Such responsibility brings in some elements of accountability. In August 2014, Ministry of Tourism had launched the Comprehensive Sustainable Tourism Criteria for India (STCI) for Accommodation, Tour Operators and Beaches, Backwaters, Lakes and Rivers sectors. It is necessary to review these criteria in the context changing situation and to devise ways for their proper implementation.

The only thing that can be said with certainty about the future is that nothing can be said with certainty. Recovery outlook, according to UNWTO remains cautious. Its panel of experts expect revival to happen only in 2022 at the earliest. 43 percent of experts expect return to the level of 2019 by 2023 while 41 percent believe it will be only in 2024 or later.

"When the sea is rough, the wise fisherman mends his nets" so goes a saying in the fishing community in the coastal areas. There is much wisdom in this common sense.

13

TOURISM: THE UNCARED-FOR PILLAR OF DEVELOPMENT[11]

"Private sector is the key mover for tourism and it is essential to create a strong, meaningful and constructive Public-Private Partnership mechanism that facilitates constant and continuous interaction. In creating a total and unique tourism experience the local community plays a vital role. And for inclusive growth participation of the community in management of destinations is essential."

The tourism industry has been greatly enthused by the description of tourism as an important pillar of development by PM Narendra Modi. There was a time in India when tourism development was seen primarily as a means to getting much-needed foreign exchange for the country. That perception has now changed. Globally, as in India, tourism is recognised as an instrument to achieve the greater goal of inclusive growth. It is significant that the pandemic ravaged tourism industry celebrated Tourism Day 2021 on the theme of Tourism for Inclusive Growth. The celebration of a day is intended to create awareness and spur committed, continuous and persistent action. Unfortunately, quite often it becomes a one-day event to be quickly forgotten.

---

11. BW Hotelier, 27 October, 2021.

In fact, the entire focus of Millennium Development Goals was on inclusive growth. MDG's progress was haphazard and SDG has reshaped and redesigned that objective in 17 goals. According to UNWTO, contribution of tourism is implicit in most of the goals and mentioned specifically in Goal 8 referring to "sustainable tourism that creates jobs and promote local culture and products". Globally, World Travel and Tourism Council estimates, by 2030 travel and tourism's share in direct employment will grow to 11.2 percent and GDP contribution to 10.9 percent. India Brand Equity Foundation (IBEF) estimates that in 2020, the Indian tourism sector accounted for 31.8 million jobs, which was 7.3 percent of the total employment in the country. By 2029, it is expected to account for about 53 million jobs. Such direct economic contribution and earning of Rs 211,611 crore of foreign exchange before Covid-19, indeed makes tourism a very strong economic activity of the country. And there is much more to talk about – contribution to preservation of art, culture and heritage, ecosystems, cuisines, craft, women's empowerment. The list is long and the story is endless.

Unfortunately, that is only half of the story and the bigger story is not often seen or appreciated. The indirect impact of tourism is much wider and extensive and that impact – call it multiplier effect or "ripple effect" – is difficult to capture in statistics. UN system of Tourism Satellite Accounts, also adopted in India, devises a way of considering all the indirect economic effects of tourism. But it is a difficult task, accuracy depends on the availability of data and their proper allocation. WTTC, for example, has shown that there are at least 30 activities at the core of tourism of which only five or six like accommodation, transportation, food and beverages, attractions management are generally visible to people. That, in fact, is like the tip of the iceberg.

Therefore, UNWTO very aptly says that behind every number there is a person. As the numbers are hazy the face of that person that tourism sustains seem also to recede to the background. And herein is the basic contradiction tourism suffering from – 'between the idea and the reality', between awareness of its tremendous economic impact and the lack of attention to nurture it. The experience of the traumatic two years of the pandemic so far reflects this contradiction.

The complete story of the ravages of the pandemic is yet to be known but it is feared that about 32 million people might have already been pushed to extreme poverty around the world. Globally, as in India, around 80 percent of the industry is composed of SMEs and it has been roughly estimated that 21.5 million might have lost jobs in tourism industry in India. They needed some very simple support to survive and recoup – liquidity support, income, payroll support when business was down to zero because of circumstances beyond their control, exemption from statutory dues for the period that business was shut due to state directives and so on. These were action consistent with the objective of inclusive growth, and they would have given much greater return to the economy in the long run. Perhaps in the concern for the bigger picture, the small picture got lost. The support that tourism industry got is much delayed, sporadic and ad hoc, not amounting to any comprehensive plan for tourism recovery.

This experience has shown once again that this important pillar of development needs to be put on firm footing. That can be done both at policy and implementation levels. Ministry of Tourism for example, depends on other ministries like Civil Aviation, Culture, Home and Surface Transport, for implementation of policies relating to tourism promotion. Such coordination takes time and often policies and implementation get delayed and the Ministry of Tourism experiences helplessness. It would be ideal if a Cabinet Committee under the chairmanship of the PM could look after tourism development and coordination. That would carry a strong message about the importance attached to tourism by the government.

The other stakeholders on whom the quality of the tourism experience and inclusive growth of tourism depend are—the state governments, the private entrepreneurs and the community. Implementation of the policies rest primarily with the state governments. The state governments should also adopt such a system of coordination and monitoring at the state level. However, the private sector is the key mover for tourism and it is essential to create a strong, meaningful and constructive Public-Private Partnership mechanism that facilitates constant and continuous interaction. In creating a total and unique tourism experience the local community plays a vital role. And for inclusive growth participation of the community in management of destinations is essential. It would be helpful to constitute a Tourism Development Committee in every district and to link sustainable and responsible tourism planning and management to the process of decentralised development.

In post-covid world the challenges for tourism are daunting, but the potential is immense if we take good care of the Pillar.

14

END OF THE TUNNEL? — AND A TIME FOR REFLECTION[12]

The most volatile commodity and the most important element shaping the future will be trust and confidence.

"It is undeniable that between recognising tourism as a pillar of development and giving it its due in the policy, there is a big gap. The policies and practices in government should be more constructive to support its pivotal role in employment generation and inclusive growth"

After two years of gloom and despair, for tourism and hospitality industry April came with fresh winds of hope, not as the "cruellest month" as Eliot had famously said. As many parts of the country celebrated and ushered in the New Year, emerging trends brought cheer and good tidings.

According to JLL momentum report, the Revenue Per Available Room (RevPAR) witnessed a growth of 100.3 percent year-on-year (YoY) — a remarkable recovery from the reported drop of national average occupancy of hotels by 48 percent, the Average Daily Rate (ADR) drop of 34 percent and the 66 percent drop in RevPAR in the fiscal year 2021. Global hospitality data analysis agency STR has been quoted as "India's hotel industry eclipsed pre-pandemic comparable

12. BW Hotelier, 17 May, 2022.

in occupancy and average daily rate (ADR) for three consecutive days during the second week of April." Reportedly domestic air travel is back growing to 10.5 m in April — a year on growth of 83 percent and only 5 percent less than the pre-Covid-19 level. In fact, the same report also says that international passenger traffic for Indian carriers witnessed a surge to 185 mn. even surpassing the pre-Covid-19 level. The combined effect of all these developments if sustained, is bound to boost travel and hospitality sector sooner and stronger than anticipated few months back.

Such time of good news however should also be a time for reflection on the lessons learnt during the bad times and also for discussions on the tasks for both the industry and the government on the road ahead. We are indeed living in an age of uncertainty and such constant worry about the future means that the industry cannot take anything for granted. The industry must be alert to the slightest wind of change in the atmosphere. For example, in an interesting article about the crumbling of "third party cookies" – of Google, Apple etc – Kurt Weinsheimer of Sojourn says that for hotels, the elimination of third-party cookies may seem scary. But a vigilant management can turn it into an opportunity to "to build more authentic relationships with guests using less intrusive methods... enabling hotels to move beyond antiquated techniques to create a personalised experience that inspires travellers to book."

The most volatile commodity and the most important element shaping the future will be trust and confidence. Confidence has been certainly growing aided by extensive vaccination and increasing public awareness and safety consciousness. Still, the uncertainty lingers. Shanghai, for example, is not only an enigma but also a symbol of doubts, suspicion and fear of the uncertain.

Hospitality industry's primary role and position in the national economy rests, among others, on its capacity to create employment. Covid-19 took away, as the Minister of Tourism informed the Parliament, a staggering 2.1 crore jobs. Mahesh Vyas, managing director and CEO, Centre for Monitoring Indian Economy (CMIE), is quoted as saying that of the total labour force of 435 million in India in 2021-22, 33 million (which is 7.5 percent) were unemployed. It is logical and necessary that government policy should nurture the job creation potential of the hospitality industry. A recent report attributed to Naukri.com says that 80 percent of the job demand came from the hospitality industry. It is well known that an old survey of the government had established – and it perhaps holds good still – that the multiplier effect of employment in hospitality is four to five times that of manufacturing, agriculture or transport sectors.

The industry will have to continuously juggle in the future between use of technology, digitalisation, creating quality employment and skilling of the manpower. The bottom line, of course is productivity and revenue.

In a path-breaking event, the President of UN General Assembly recently convened a debate on "Putting sustainable and resilient tourism at the heart of an inclusive recovery". This concern for sustainable and responsible tourism has been the most overwhelming outcome of the Covid-19 experience and the hospitality industry will have to don the leadership role in the future journey. It is only appropriate that HAI has joined hands with World Travel and Tourism Council (WTTC) to promote the concept of Hotel Sustainability Basics' initiative among its member hotels. This initiative recognises set of criteria or benchmark for sustainable practices that all hotels should commit, adopt and implement. But more than acceptance of the criteria, sustainability should be the lifestyle and raison d'etre for the industry. The good examples set by the industry leaderships should flow down the line to all sections.

Much soul-searching required at the government level as well. It is undeniable that between recognising tourism as a pillar of development and giving it its due in the policy, there is a big gap. The policies and practices in government should be more constructive to support tourism's pivotal role in employment generation and inclusive growth. Why is it that when all activities were locked down and income was zero, the industry had to run from pillar to post to get the statutory dues, the fixed charges on power etc exempted or deferred? When there was no capacity to pay, resulting from their compliance of state norms on lockdown, why not the industry and particularly the vulnerable SMEs be given automatic relief in interest burden or in repayments of loans? Could not some of these 2.1 crore jobs have been saved if the government had come forward to hold hands of the employers who were trying to keep the jobs?

Time may lessen the pain of the industry of the last two unprecedented years but if the foundation of the future must be strong the lessons should not be forgotten. The future – uncertain though – is what we look forward with optimism.

The industry and the government, in an atmosphere of strong collaborative partnership should continuously discuss, debate and devise safe ways for the future and facilitate the hospitality industry to grow to its full potential and contribute to inclusive growth. Disaster management is not just limited to physical relief. More pertinent is prevention of social disaster that follows from failure to take timely remedial steps. What Albert Einstein said in a different context is so pertinent now for all the stakeholders — “Learn from yesterday, live for today, hope for tomorrow. The important thing is not to stop questioning.”

15

TOURISM REVIVAL: OPTIMISM AND WORRIES[13]

Favourable trends are showing average occupancy in the hotels as well as in average revenue per room.

"Industry analysts have considered that the recovery of the hotel sector is back on course with all the parameters like occupancy, ADR and RevPAR higher than their pre-pandemic levels. There are, however, regional variations, western and southern regions showing better results in general than the rest. These figures again are subject to seasonal variations and local conditions"

There is optimism and confidence in the air for tourism and hospitality sector, both locally and globally. The revival process is undoubtedly gathering pace with international arrivals having increased 182 percent year-on-year in Q1 2022 to an estimated 117 million international arrivals. Such strong rebound notwithstanding international tourism still remained 61 percent below the pre-pandemic level.

The good news, however, is the apparent return of confidence in travel. The latest UNWTO Confidence Index survey indicates that 81 percent of tourism professionals see better prospects for 2022 and

13. BW Hotelier, 03 September, 2022.

that a higher number of experts (48 percent) now see a potential return of international arrivals to 2019 levels in 2023.

However, as expected domestic tourism has been the main driver of tourism growth in 2022. The estimated domestic passenger's load factor is reported to be around 85 percent as against 49 percent in May 2021 and 90 percent in May 2019. This implies that domestic tourism is almost back to pre-pandemic level. As the economy gathers steam, the threat of Covid-19 recedes and confidence returns, domestic tourism is sure to surge ahead.

The favourable trends are showing in average occupancy in the hotels as well as in average revenue per room. In brief, industry analysts have considered that the recovery of the hotel sector is back on course with all the parameters like occupancy, ADR and RevPAR higher than their pre-pandemic levels. There are, however, regional variations, western and southern regions showing better results in general than the rest. These figures again are subject to seasonal variations and local conditions.

As optimism returns and the tourism and hospitality sector recovers, it is a time to think of major policy initiatives on two fronts. First, learning lessons from the pandemic, to prepare against future shocks – like economic safety net for the vulnerable sections, greater coordination among the states on health and travel protocols as well as on relief measures.

Second urgent action needed to meet the future challenges, of sustainability, of creating accommodation by according incentives like infrastructure status, expanding access to destinations and spreading destinations to ease carrying capacity and so on. For example, the distribution of tourists, domestic and international, is rather skewed so far. The top 10 states/ UTs get 87.2 percent of foreign tourists and 87 percent of domestic visits. The other 26 states/ UTs receive on an average 0.5 percent of arrivals.

While the signs of recovery are very optimistic, there are worries and uncertainties too. Occasional recurrence of the virus in different parts of the world, still uncertain behaviour of the monkey pox, the volatile global geo-political situation and looming threat of recession in major economies like USA always keep the industry on its toes. It is also necessary to keep abreast of the emerging trends in the world and their likely impact on India. With the festival season approaching the demand is expected to surge and the tendency to relax on health and safety protocols may be strong. The hospitality sector should set an example in not relaxing at all on the health precautions and insisting on observance of the protocols by the travellers.

Airbnb is reportedly introducing a new concept of "live and work anywhere". It combines the changed work process "unfettered to office" with the desire and requirement of leisure. According to Airbnb the scheme is working well in non-metro areas where local communities drive down to nearby locations for work and long stay. It is happening in India too. If it gains momentum, it may change the complexion of tourism in the country and spread tourism to hitherto unexplored destinations and locations.

The new trend of working brought in by the pandemic, facilitated by rapid advances in technology, making it possible to combine leisure with pleasure and work, is defining travel in more ways than one. The workstation idea perhaps will change business travel considerably. Accor CEO has said that while their business is booming and Paris is on "fire", 20-25 percent of business travellers are not coming back and perhaps will never come back. Staycation and leisure tourism rule the roost now.

In many countries, hotels are facing shortage of staff to service the customers. In Europe and elsewhere, the most disturbing post-Covid-19 experience has been labour shortage, caused by people who moved due to closure or decline of business or people moving jobs looking for better options. Accor, for example, reported a loss of about 15 percent labour. The severe impact of labour shortage on the civil aviation services in Europe has been widely reported. In hospitality, some industry stalwarts have termed it as a "wakeup" call to look at working pattern, pay, nature of staffing and management structures.

It has been mentioned that the younger generation are neither attached to fixed jobs nor are enthused by traditional concept of loyalty and look for flexibility. Some of the reported figures are indeed worrying. One report says that Spain where tourism accounts for 13 percent of economic activity and Portugal with 15 percent are experiencing shortage of 200,000 and 15,000 workers respectively. Similar reports say that to overcome such problems Europe's largest hotel chain, Accor is experimenting with recruitment of people without any past experience.

As the future unfolds there will perhaps be continuous experimentation to find solutions to emerging challenges. As Friedrich Nietzsche said "the future influences the present just as much as the past".

16

RECOVERY TRENDS IN HOSPITALITY INDUSTRY[14]

Hospitality industry is again daring to dream. Logistics Analysis and Research Consultants, a research and analysis outfit estimates that RevPAR will increase by 18 percent during 2022. JLL, another hospitality analysis organisation says that the Indian hospitality sector witnessed a rapid and strong recovery post the third wave in January 2022, driven by growth in demand for leisure, wedding, and business travel.

In the beginning of the new millennium a series of geopolitical and natural events rocked the tourism and hospitality industry, for the first time stopping the unbroken story of growth of five decades. Tsunami, 9/11, SAARS, Global Financial meltdown - all shattered tourism but there was optimism that tourism, fuelled by man's eternal urge to wander, will bounce back. So it did. UNWTO's long term forecast issued in 2010 indicated that the 1.4 billion tourist arrival mark would be reached in 2020, "International Tourist Arrivals Reach 1.4 billion Two Years Ahead of Forecast" proudly announced a report of UNWTO in early 2019.

Then came the catastrophe-Covid-19 Pandemic pushing back tourism by 30 years. So total was the helplessness of human action,

14. ET Hospitality World, June 22, 2022.

so widespread was the despair, that expectations about the future was muted at best. However, halfway through to 2022 there are all indications that tourism is back - not yet quite to the pre-pandemic level but expecting to be there by the end of the year or by early next year. Hospitality industry is again daring to dream. Logistics Analysis and Research Consultants, a research and analysis outfit estimates that RevPAR will increase by 18 percent during 2022. JLL, another hospitality analysis organisation says that the Indian hospitality sector witnessed a rapid and strong recovery post the third wave in January 2022, driven by growth in demand for leisure, wedding, and business travel. As a result, Revenue Per Available Room (RevPAR) witnessed a growth of 39.1 percent year-on-year (YoY) in Q1, 2022 (Jan-March).

The reaction of the customers to the massive disruption to travel for two years has been mixed and varied. In general, people are dying to go out but old habits of travel have changed. These changes have been much talked about and can be broadly summed up. Choice of people is driven by the degree of confidence in the service providers, the assurance about health and safety norms, and by the concern for sustainable practices. A report attributed to Booking.com says that as per their survey, in 2020, 96 percent of Indian travellers identified sustainable travel as important to them, while 76 percent said they were more determined to make sustainable choices when looking to travel again in the future. It is a remarkably high percentage of people taking sustainability seriously. Before the Covid, some surveys by UNWTO had established that about 30 percent of travellers travel only for environmental interests and about the same number of people take sustainable standards of the service providers in the destinations very seriously in making a choice.

Covid changed the working environment and practices and technology made it possible to quickly adapt to the new norm of "online" work. The resultant eruption of demand for "staycation"- people mixing new norms of work with travel not too far from home is one of the most significant developments of post-covid tourism.

Hospitality industry in the coming days must be attuned to these changes, some of them quite visible others not so perceptible but slowly influencing the trends. Hotels will need innovative use of technical tools to build that confidence in customer's mind, with greater connect to the customers, yet lesser physical connection. Technology and digitisation have made it possible to have increasing personalisation of services - personalised assurances of health and safety needs, of a home away from home, an office away from office. Use of technology for personalised contact with the customers provides an opportunity to stay ahead of the competition as well. Hospitality industry will need to contend with the fact that technology also empowers the customer, with more options and choices about price, product, quality, service and a host of other issues.

Similarly, the response of the industry to the customers growing concern for sustainability, must be of substance and visible, open to scrutiny not just ideological commitment. JLL's survey of the industry for 2022 points out that the industry can derive substantial benefits in terms of higher asset values, decreasing operational costs and increased consumer demand by putting substance to sustainability commitment.

In this initial period of recovery, some writers have mentioned the emergence of a global trend for all-inclusive brand resort hotels. Sally French, writing in NerdWallet calls 2022 the year of 'all-inclusive' travel -citing the example of Hyatt's acquisition of Apple Leisure Group (making more than 100 new resorts under Hyatt brand) and Marriott acquiring 20 properties under a new brand dubbed "All inclusive by Marriott Bonvoy". It will be of interest to watch how this trend develops and how it affects the Indian market.

Hospitality industry is also quite concerned about the impact of "skill- gaps" faced all over the world. As Dobbs, Manyika and Woetzel in the book "No Ordinary Disruption" tracing the global forces breaking the trends point out the story of skill gaps coexisting with high unemployment is not new. They had estimated that by 2020 the world may have a gap of 85 million skilled and semi-skilled workers alongside a surplus of 95 m low skilled workers. Much before the pandemic, in 2014, USA, long suffering from chronic unemployment had 4.8 million skilled job openings. The problem has been exacerbated by the loss of job during the pandemic and skilled persons moving away to look for better opportunities. Companies are trying to overcome this problem by changing inhouse skilling, upgradation of existing skill, encouraging multi-skilling and so on. Research has shown that use of technology can improve the productivity of existing skilled workers by 20 percent and smart technology along with a bit of training can equip low skill workers to perform high skill jobs. The need for skilled persons is going to be more important in coming days of increasing use of technology and therefore it will be a challenge to innovative use of technology and smart management practices.

In some parts of the world the hospitality industry has faced supply chain problems. An industry which consumes such wide range of goods and services will be vulnerable to uncertainties of global geo-political and economic situations like increasing inflation. Supply chain issues will need constant and close monitoring, advance planning, innovations to save on use of resources.

There is much enthusiasm about a robust revival, much excitement about uncertain future challenges bringing out the best of Indian hospitality industry. After all, as an African proverb goes - "smooth seas do not make skilful sailors".

17

THE UNION BUDGET CAN BOOST TOURISM AND HOSPITALITY REVIVAL[15]

The tale of last two years for the tourism and hospitality industry has been a tale of unprecedented woes. It is also a story of great resilience of the industry, its capacity to adapt and to innovate.

The Tourism and Hospitality sector, a significant contributor to the country's growth narrative-earning valuable foreign exchange, creating jobs, helping inclusive growth earnestly looks to the government to facilitate its revival. The full extent of the damage is yet to be known but the broad contours have been well reported. Nearly 40 percent of hotels were reported to be on the brink of closure. In a sector providing almost 10 percent of global employment, 70 percent of jobs are at risk. As is well known, in 2019, Tourism & Hospitality sector contributed USD 194 billion to the Indian economy, accounting for 6.8 percent of GDP and 8 percent of employment. The hotel sector's contribution to GDP shrunk by 47 percent in Q1 of 2021. The nationwide average daily rate (ADR) saw, a drop of 34 percent. The ripple effect throughout the economy, with countless craftspeople, skilled chefs, hotel staff, artisans, tourist guides, and feeder industries

15. ET Hospitality World, Jan 7, 2022.

like transport, railways, aviation, is enormous and the enormity is not often captured in official statistics. The uncertainty has resulted in flip-flop of bookings and cancellations.

Against such a grim background the crippled industry has been seeking government support to be on its feet-in the form of liquidity support, moratoriums, rationalisation of taxes among others. At this crucial stage of revival, the industry has articulated in its submission to the Finance Ministry with some vital fiscal reforms and removal of illogical procedural roadblocks.

For example, to make global standard hotel accommodation overhauling and facelift of room interiors are needed, every 2-3 years, requiring huge investments. Yet, while expenditure in Plant and Machinery is allowed depreciation at 15-20 percent, building costs, that comprise 70 percent of the hotel costs, only get depreciation at the rate of 10 percent. The industry seeks the benefits under Section 35AD (for deduction of capital expenditure for greenfield projects) to be available from the date the business commences, even though the classification certificate is issued much later and similar benefits to be extended to hotels undergoing reconstruction, or for brownfield projects of above INR 50 crore.

The prescribed and lower rate of 17.16 percent tax under Section 115BAB applicable to new manufacturing companies can be extended to production of food, and a clarification to the end may be provided. When the future is unmistakably in digitalisation, it is necessary to review the TDS provision, under Section 1940, which creates a responsibility on the hotel to withhold tax at source at the rate 1 percent on the number of sales of goods/services made through the hotel/hotel group website. This section should be exempted for the Hotel Operators which are providing reservation facilities to its own branded hotel/Network Hotels or a suitable clarification should be provided in this regard.

Hotels feel that Section 269ST, that puts restrictions on receipt of cash from foreign tourists exceeding INR 1,99,999 is inconsistent with the intent and spirit of this provision to curb black money in

India. Foreigners should therefore be exempted from this provision and there should be no limit on cash accepted by hotels in foreign currency from foreigners as payment for services rendered.

For the immediate future domestic tourism will be the catalyst for tourism recovery. To incentivize domestic tourism, the government should modify Leave Travel Allowance (LTA) rules, allowing LTA to be claimed for expenses incurred on hotel stays in addition to travel expenses. Tax breaks on travel and hotel stays should be available to all employees whether in the government sector or private. Making LTA benefits available annually instead of block years will also boost domestic tourism.

At a time when business loss is the order of the day and uncertainty in business looms, it makes sense to amend the Income Tax Act (Section 72) so that business losses are allowed to be carried forward for up to 12 years, instead of eight financial years. A change is needed in the I-T law to allow such write downs either as "capital loss" or "business loss", provided regulatory approvals are obtained for such write-offs.

Alcohol Sales are a good revenue earner and the demand to remove it from the excise category, and to place under the GST net will help the revenue recovery process. It will be a great incentive to the hospitality industry and a big boost to country's foreign exchange earnings to increase the current rate of rewards, at 5 percent, Under the Service Export from India Scheme (SEIS), to 10 percent for the next three to four years. The demand of the industry that foreign exchange earnings should be treated at par with other exports and services and accorded "Deemed Export of Services" (as considered in the IT sector), along with a zero rate on GST is logical and reasonable.

The government's pragmatic policy of tourism revival through domestic tourism would require extensive investment in mid-market and budget tourist accommodation outside the metro cities. Providing Infrastructure Status to Hospitality industry and declaring hotel projects of above INR 25 crore capex (excluding land) as infrastructure would spur activities for accommodation as well as much needed economic investments. The RBI had recognised Hotels as a sub-sector of Social Infrastructure. But the infrastructure status was granted to projects above Rs 200 crore leaving out the much-needed investments in non-metro areas.

Government have taken many bold steps for ease of doing business and tourism and hospitality should not be left behind. It would be a great progressive step to create a "Single Window Clearance" for many licences required in the sector and also to increase the timeline for licences from annual to 3/5 years.

Hospitality sector flourishes best when overall tourism burgeons. By all account Indian tourism is yet away from its full potential. Hotel Association of India has been persistently advocating for effective policy interventions like infrastructure status for hospitality, benefits of "industry", creating an empowered National Tourism Board, robust Public-Private Partnership mechanism, rationalisation of GST, GST set off for MICE held in offsite location-just to mention a few. It is now the right time to take such bold policy decisions to launch Indian tourism into the new world of opportunities.

Most of the recommendations of the tourism and hospitality sector require only marginal adjustment in policies to facilitate seamless growth. They do not have much financial implications either. For the government, the reforms requested are small but for the industry they may be the catalyst for big growth. The country looks forward to the next budget to lay the foundation for that big growth. In a sense the words of Nobel Peace Prize Winner Desmond Tutu are pertinent here- "My humanity is bound up in yours, for we can only be human together." All sectors of the economy are interconnected. If tourism and hospitality, described as a pillar of development by the PM, is firmly integrated into the structure for country's economic rejuvenation, it can be a game changer.

18

HOSPITALITY—BUSINESS AS USUAL?[16]

Disruptive experiences often lead to innovations and so it happened in hospitality industry also. And aided by ebbing of the pandemic, extensive vaccination coverage reviving consumer confidence, easing of travel restrictions the year 2022 arrived with a lot of hope for this sector and the hospitality industry is back on its "Road to Recovery."

The hospitality sector has been through a roller-coaster ride for the last two years. The pandemic has affected the entire ecosystem of the industry like never before. The severity of the impact has not yet been fully assessed but a few statistics that have been shared in public may illustrate its magnitude. Union Minister for Tourism and Culture, G Kisan Reddy, informed the Parliament that 14.5 million jobs in the sector had been lost in the first wave of Covid-19 infection, 5.2 million and 1.8 million during the second wave and the third wave respectively. A Hotelivate report says that in the fiscal 2021 nationwide average occupancy of hotels dropped by 48 percent over the earlier year and the Average Daily Rate (ADR) saw a drop of 34 percent. The revenue per available room had a staggering drop of 66 percent.

The redeeming feature in this gloom was that the industry showed a lot of resilience to survive. Disruptive experiences often lead to innovations and so it happened in hospitality industry also. And aided by ebbing of the pandemic, extensive vaccination coverage reviving consumer confidence, easing of travel restrictions the year 2022 arrived with a lot of hope for this sector and the hospitality industry is back on its "Road to Recovery".

16. ET Hospitality World, May 5, 2022.

According to a recent JLL momentum report, the revenue per available room (RevPAR) witnessed a growth of 100.3 percent year-on-year (YoY). The report also echoes the general industry feeling that the demand for domestic leisure travel, staycations, workcations, leisure travel, destination weddings, holidays and festivals will be the prime factors accelerating business recovery. These are happy signs, and the recovery outlook is in tune with the cautious optimism of UNWTO expressed earlier. Its panel of experts expected revival to happen only in 2022 at the earliest 43 percent of experts expected return to the level of 2019 by 2023 while 41 percent believed it will be only in 2024 or later.

As the industry looks forward to recovery and better days ahead, trends that are setting the stage now and likely to do so in the future are getting clearer, globally and in India too. Confidence, as often said, is the new currency and the covid shake up has made it imperative that there will be no compromise on health and safety protocols. In the initial stages of recovery, the pent-up demand is expected to push prices. But digital savvy consumers, having the tools to weigh more options to compare and choose, will demand unique experiences, expect flexibility in booking and refunds, and thereby raise the industry bar on competitiveness. Above all increasing consumer awareness about sustainability and the lessons starkly taught by the pandemic will make demand for sustainable norms in service delivery a prerequisite, putting greater responsibility on the service providers. In short, it will no longer be business as usual.

No wonder that the theme of CII's national conference for 21-22 had aptly summed up the issues for a "future ready India". Competitiveness, Growth, Sustainability, Technology."

Technology is likely to have so pervasive an influence on business that that it should have a closer and continuous attention of the industry. A Feb 2020 survey by a World Bank Group established a correlation between 'Digital Platforms and the Demand for International Tourism Services.' The National Digital Tourism Mission sees digitisation in tourism sector presenting opportunities for tourism enterprises to expand their market reach, increase growth, improve operational efficiencies, and sharpen their competitive edge. Over the long term, it says, digital transformation can unlock innovation and ensure the competitiveness of India's tourism sector.

Technology changes fast. It requires new look at skilling of the manpower and continuous upgradation to keep up with the changes. The hospitality industry is not uniform in its capacity to adapt to changes and skilling. A very large component of the industry—the small and medium sector, located in the non-metro stations, will have inherent disadvantages in gearing up to the challenges.

Elsewhere in the world the industry is facing another problem-of staff shortages. A WTTC report says that while supply and demand are set to adjust gradually during 2022, the problem is likely to remain. To ensure that it does not become a long-term problem, the Report underlines the importance for businesses and governments alike to implement and sustain policies that facilitate among others, upskill and reskill the workforce, and promote education and apprenticeships. A recent report by naukri.com says March 2022 has seen up to 82 percent hiring in the hospitality sector. The report however must be seen in proper perspective - it signifies, as expected that hospitality sector is spurring employment growth - 82 percent of the demand coming from the sector but that percentage may be miniscule of the total jobs lost.

Hopefully the revival trends will hold good and hospitality sector will again be a driver in India's economic recovery. But many nagging questions will remain to be asked so that the spectre of the pandemic do not haunt the industry again. In case of any future disaster will the industry particularly the small and medium sections, have to run from pillar to post to clutch to the survival straws? Will the industry and the government think of some future social security umbrella for the most vulnerable?

There is much wisdom in the old saying that when you are thirsty, it's too late to think about digging a well. We may as well heed what the Roman statesman Marcus Tullius Cicero said in 100 B.C. "Let us not go over the old ground. Let us rather prepare for what is to come."

19

RESHAPING INBOUND TOURISM[17]

It is necessary to rebrand India, not only remodelling and relaunching Incredible India but also projecting a safe and secure India that inspires confidence in the travellers.

In a recent statement the Minister of Tourism had announced the goal of 15 million foreign tourist arrivals by 2024. Domestic travel had so well fuelled tourism revival in India post-Covid, that inbound tourism had for some time receded to the background. In any case time was not yet opportune to concentrate on inbound tourism as the world was not yet fully ready. The UNWTO Confidence Index survey indicated that one percent of tourism professionals see better prospects for international travels in 2022 but 48 percent of experts see a potential return of international arrivals to 2019 levels only in 2023. It is now time to prepare for that revival and prepare a long-term inbound tourism promotion policy that is in tune with the new realities, opportunities and challenges.

There are optimistic signs too to support the Ministry's expectations of growth. There are reports that domestic air travel is back to pre-Covid level. The international arrivals jumped by 177 percent in March 2022 as compared to March 2021. Data from the ministry of tourism shows that 3,263,219 foreign tourist arrivals (FTAs) have been registered this year through the month of August,

17. ET Hospitality World, Dec 7, 2022.

which is 47.2 percent of the 6,914,987 foreign visitors' arrival during the same period in 2019. However, 2021 had seen a decline of 45 percent over 2020 and 2020 had seen a massive 75 percent decline. So, the present growth only shows that the situation is slowly getting back to normal, but not fully as yet. It is also not clear how much of the arrival is NRIs coming home. Generally, NRIs make for about 35 to 40 percent of total international arrivals to India and in 2021 out of 7 mn. arrivals 5.5 m were NRIs.

Nevertheless, it is now time for reshaping inbound tourism. It is necessary to rebrand India, not only remodelling and relaunching Incredible India but also projecting a safe and secure India that inspires confidence in the travellers. Technology has empowered the consumers to have greater choice options and in that consumer choice, ease and cost of travel will be primary factors. Government initiative to attract foreign tourists by providing one-month free tourist visa to 5,00,000 tourists until end of March 2022 was a good gesture but it is likely that the circumstances at that time and the level of confidence for travel might have outweighed the advantages of the initiative. As travel picks up, it may be worthwhile to revisit the scheme as a measure of incentive. Similarly, government have extended e-visa facility to 156 countries till date. A close look at the tourists' feedback on this scheme and also the visa on arrival scheme will go a long way in influencing consumer choice in favour of India.

Air seat capacity and cost are other important factors that influence decisions to travel to a particular destination. By 2037, 520 million people are expected to travel to, from, or within India, according to statistics from Invest India.

There are reports from reliable agencies that air seat capacity and the targets of international arrivals do not match. Apparently, this is an area that should merit close attention of the government and a realistic and holistic picture of tourism targets and aviation capabilities should be in the interest of Indian tourism. Internally there is good news as the government plans to build 100 airports by 2024, under the UDAN Scheme in order to accommodate India's expanding passenger demand.

A recent Google survey has shown, as indeed have several similar surveys, that as the locked-up aspirations for travel create a surge, among other things cultural engagements and sensitivity to sustainable concerns will weigh with the travellers. India's enormous cultural wealth, its variety gives the country an edge over many others.

India's presidentship of the G-20 is a great boon for tourism at a time when international tourism is picking up. It will give a year-round focus on India and that focus can be the foundation for a long-term tourism growth. As the events take place in different parts of the country, the participants—all important policy-makers and opinion leaders - will have an opportunity to savour the excellence and variety of Indian tourism products and services. G-20 should be used as an opportunity to build infrastructure like accommodation and transport in those destinations across the country where various events take place and make these destinations future ready. In that context the long-standing demand of HAI to grant infrastructure status to hospitality sector becomes very relevant and should receive priority attention of the government. In essence the G-20 showcasing of tourism could recall the motto Nehru had used in the early years of Indian tourism - "welcome a tourist and send back a friend".

The world celebrated the Tourism Day last year on the theme of "rethinking tourism"-putting people and planet first. Last year, for the first time in its history, the United Nations discussed tourism with the objective of "Putting sustainable and resilient tourism at the heart of an inclusive recovery" and appealed to the nations to renew political commitment to support tourism as an engine of inclusive growth. PM Modi has often described tourism which provides the highest employment, as a pillar of development and Mahatma Gandhi had described tourism as "the language of peace" -which is one of the objectives that G-20 under India's presidentship intends to pursue.

It is only logical that resurgence of Indian tourism and hospitality- the vision@47-should be founded on an acceptance of this role of tourism and hospitality and putting tourism in its due place in nation building. The rest will follow.

20

EXPANDING THE HORIZON OF EXPERIENCE[18]

Wellness, as a tourism resource, is not a very old concept though the tradition behind it is ancient. The Covid-19 crisis was a watershed moment in the development of tourism, compelling stakeholders to look at sustainable ways to rebuild tourism, and to look at opportunities for transformation. "Wellness" is one way of such transformation.

"Tourism is difficult to define... but in general a tourist is a temporarily leisured person who voluntarily visits a place away from home for the purpose of experiencing a change," writes Valene L Smith in a delightful book "Hosts and Tourists: The Anthropology of Tourism". This definition combines two important aspects of modern tourism: "experience" and "change".

Towards the end of the last century economists explained that we were entering a new age of "experience economy". The experience economy—a term coined by economists B. Joseph Pine II and James H. Gilmore in 1998—is the selling of memorable experiences to customers. They explained that it was the next frontier, following the agricultural, then industrial then service economies and the next generation of consumers—millennials—would prefer compelling

18. Engage, HAI, Vol. 3, Issue 3, May-June 2023.

experiences. About the same time, UNWTO assessed the future megatrends and said that the focus of tourism was shifting to delivery of "unique experiences".

After a journey of quarter of a century it can be said that these mega trends continue to be relevant. These emerging trends had implications for management of tourism and hospitality. The most important impact was that tourism was becoming what was described as "a market of one". The consumer, empowered by fast-changing technology, with more options and choices at his disposal, expects unique experiences. Serving that experience requires imagination, personal attention and professional competence. The quality and content of human resource development also require to be changed to meet the service quality needed to create such an experience.

"Wellness" in that sense is an important component of creating unique experiences. Wellness, as a tourism resource, is not a very old concept though the tradition behind it is ancient. The Covid-19 crisis was a watershed moment in the development of tourism, compelling stakeholders to look at sustainable ways to rebuild tourism, and to look at opportunities for transformation. "Wellness" is one way of such transformation.

The first Tourism Policy of 1982, the high-level National Tourism Committee, and the National Action Plan of 1992, did not make any specific mention of "wellness" as a tourism product. The first indirect reference was made in the National Tourism Policy of 2002. It provides the essence of what is wellness: "India is today being rediscovered by the world for the depth of its understanding of physical, mental, emotional and spiritual manifestations of the world and humankind. ....this can be India's most unique tourism product—holistic healing and rejuvenation of the individual from every dimension—physical, mental, emotional and spiritual, and in doing so, it will capture the essence of the best of Indian philosophy and culture." However, the concept was not developed further nor the roadmap for exploiting this "unique" advantage was charted.

The Draft Tourism Policy of 2021, in a section on product-specific roadmaps, clubs Ayurveda/Holistic Health Systems/Wellness together but there seems to be some lack of clarity still. It says: "There is increasing consumer demand for wellness services and products the world over. Wellness also brings in high yield tourists and significantly increases the average duration of stay." At the same time, the Draft also mentions spirituality, Yoga and Medical Tourism as other components of tourism promotion.

It is essential to remember while thinking of leveraging this unique advantage, that wellness is not just yoga or ayurvedic treatment. It is a comprehensive totality of holistic healing and mental, physical, emotional, spiritual, and cultural well-being. Managing such a wide canvas is difficult and often therefore attention gets limited to parts of it only. Considering the importance of the concept in a world ravaged by Covid and now desperately looking for lifestyle that is more in tune with nature and sustainable, it will be appropriate to design a proper policy to develop wellness tourism.

At the same time wellness tourism should not be seen in isolation. Its development should fit into what the finance minister described in the budget speech as "an integrated and innovative approach". In fact, the National Action Plan of 1992 also talked about the integrated growth of tourism, but it was conceived in terms of creating circuits rather than providing integrated services and experiences within a destination. From that point of view the approach enunciated in the budget to develop every destination "as a complete package" makes much sense. Wellness tourism should first be integrated within the destination with other tourism experiences and then it should be integrated within the circuit. Such complementarities will enhance the total experience of the tourist.

The components of wellness tourism are derived from long traditions of the country and are unique to India. It is essential to ensure the authenticity of this experience. It is quite likely that as the demand increases there will be temptation to fill up the supply by people and organisations who do not have the expertise to create that authentic experience. Considering the very nature of the product which can impact health and well-being of a person unless done properly, governments have a responsibility to oversee the competence and expertise of the service providers. It is heartening to note that the Ministry of Tourism is alive to such concerns. The Ministry of Tourism has drafted guidelines for wellness tourism that address issues regarding making available quality publicity material, training and capacity-building for the service providers etc. Guidelines for Accreditation of wellness centers also have been developed by National Board for Accreditation of Hospitals & Healthcare Services (NABH) in consultation with AYUSH.

The National Tourism Policy 2002 enunciates the following at the beginning:

- India is a journey of mind and soul
- It is a journey of the five senses
- It is a journey of self-discovery
- It is a journey of self-fulfillment.

Wellness tourism has immense potential in a world looking for such journeys. It is now time to package it imaginatively, promote it vigorously and service it professionally to satisfy the tourists' thirst for unique experiences.

21

Carving a Niche in Medical Tourism![19]

India has gained a reputation in delivering quality medical services. Owing to travel being on the backfoot during the pandemic, there was a huge reduction in incoming medical tourists to India. MP Bezbaruah, Secretary General, Hotel Association India (HAI), suggests how this sector can now be revived.

According to the Union Ministry of Tourism (MOT), India is ranked 10th in the Medical Tourism Index (MTI) for 2020-21 among 46 countries. India attracts 1 percent of international travellers annually, though the scope of expansion in medical tourism is immense. There is an increase in foreign visitors arriving for medical reasons from 1.83 lakh in 2021 to 3.05 lakh in 2022. Currently, the Indian medical value travel market is US$ 5-6 billion and is expected to reach US$ 13 billion by 2026. The rising expense of healthcare in foreign countries is a consequence of the Ukraine-Russia war. The escalated interest in medical tourism has called for various governmental initiatives like Heal in India, the creation of an e-Visa for Ayush, and accreditation of Ayush.

Current status

While medical visas or M-visas facilitate Foreign Tourist Arrivals (FTAs) in the country, the private hospital chains, branded as hospital destinations, are attracting medical tourists by providing facilities, niche offerings, and customised luxury. Top hospitals have been

19. Trav Talk, May 2023.

certified by international accreditation schemes to attract patients looking for quality care at affordable costs. Cosmetic surgery, orthopaedic surgery, cardiac surgery, and dental operations are reportedly the most popular medical procedures among foreign visitors. According to a survey by the Confederation of Indian Industry (CII), Chennai attracts 40 percent of the country's medical tourists.

Shripad Yesso Naik, Union Minister of State for Tourism, highlighted that around 1.4 million tourists visited India for medical reasons. The country has formulated a National Strategy and Roadmap for Medical and Wellness Tourism to put India on the international map. However, for its rapid growth, attention needs to be given to appropriate government regulations for patient protection, insurance frameworks, travel and visa facilitation, and other factors that influence the patient's experience and treatment outcomes.

The Edge

To attract medical tourists, maintaining global standards is a primary requisite. Thematic creatives on niche tourism products like medical tourism are being used in government campaigns to cater to diverse consumer interests. These include TV commercials on yoga, wellness, medical facilities, and infrastructure. India can also leverage on its competitive position in the pharmaceutical and biotechnology sector, where it has established a name for itself in delivering low-cost drugs and vaccines. Huge potential exists in reimagining the sector.

The overall standard of service, state-of-the-art medical facilities, pool of skilled and reputed healthcare professionals, cost effectiveness, blending of traditional healthcare and wellness practices, and diversity of tourism products and experience are several factors contributing towards attractiveness of India. According to MOT Report, majority of visitors are from the Asian and African countries. With easy availability of English-speaking service providers, and expert interpreters available at most multi-specialty private hospitals, foreign travellers feel at ease in India.

'Collaborative efforts need of the hour'

Hotel Association of India (HAI) has been engaging with the government at various levels. "HAI has always emphasised the importance of collaborative partnership with the government. Considering the well-recognised and very important role that the industry plays in employment creation and boosting inclusive growth, we have focused on policy formulations that will promote the growth and development of hotels in the long run."

Two key interventions can help the industry—"according to hotels, the status of an 'Infrastructure Industry' and allowing hotels to avail the benefits currently available for the industry. Securing infrastructure status would facilitate soft financing of hotels, reducing their gestation period making hotel investments more attractive. This will open up vast opportunities for the sector to provide employment to a wide spectrum of job seekers from the unskilled to the specialised, even in the remote parts of the country."

Similarly, the benefits of industry like lower utility tariffs, property tax and licence fees will reduce the fixed operational costs of hotels and allow them to use surpluses generated for ploughing back into the business. Both have been long-standing demands of the sector.

Pushing for infra status

"The demand has been captured and recommended by the MOT in the draft document of National Tourism Policy. It may be pertinent to mention here that in its 295th report titled 'Potential of Tourist Spots in the country – Connectivity and Outreach' placed before both the houses on 27 July 2021, the Department-related Parliamentary Standing Committee on Transport, Tourism and Culture, observes that the hospitality industry is in huge distress under the impact of the pandemic and is looking at mass unemployment and pan India bankruptcies. The committee believes that there is an imperative need to accord infrastructure status to hotel projects with capex above Rs 25 crore (excluding land) and include the same in the infrastructure lending list of the RBI. We are very hopeful of a positive development."

Issues at hand

Some of the significant isues that impact the industry are "Rationalisation of GST, shortage of skilled personnel, excessive and heavy licencing, cumbersome procedures for approvals of hotel projects, reduced reward point in of SEIS. DGFT guidelines for schemes such as EPCG need to be reviewed in light of the unprecedented situation of nil to negligible foreign exchange earnings for hotels in the last couple of years. Due to the pandemic, the Government has done a lot of work in recent years on promoting 'ease of doing business'. Bodies like RBI have recognised that the industry is amongst the most stressed and have included the sector in the ECLGS Scheme. The scheme has been extended in the Union Budget of 2022-23 and more funds have been made available to the sector under the scheme."

ECLGS Scheme

The Emergency Credit Line Guarantee Scheme (ECLGS), its recent extension up to March 2023 and earmarking of an additional Rs 50,000 crore for hospitality and related sectors have all been welcome initiatives. "The scheme should be customised and tailored to suit the unique hotel business model and future outlook for the sector."

22

THE YEAR OF HOPE AND A NEW BEGINNING[20]

The year 2023 holds even better promise but there are worries and uncertainties too.

"Domestic travel played an important role in shaping the industry in 2022. Domestic tourism has always been the most prominent feature of growth of Indian tourism and hospitality, but its integral importance for the survival and growth of the sector was perhaps never as much realised as in 2022. The year is marked by empowerment of the consumers' changes in the preferences of travellers".

The year 2022 will be one to be remembered by the hospitality industry. It started with a lot of fear and uncertainty and with abundance of hope and expectations. It ended with lot of satisfaction. By the end of the year, the industry was happily back on rails with Average Daily Rates (ADRs), RevPAR and occupancy levels back to or above the pre-pandemic levels. According to JLL's latest Q3 report, the year witnessed the growth of 89.6 percent in RevPAR from Jul-Sept'22 (Q3 2022) and RevPAR growth of 89.6 percent from Jul-Sept'22 (Q3 2022).

It is a remarkable recovery, from the dismal situation of practically zero business in 2020. But the year will be remembered for reasons

20. BW Hotelier, 01 March 2023.

more than recovery in room rates or profit. The industry can justifiably be proud of the resilience it showed during the dark days with little or no support from the government.

Globally, as in India, the Covid-19 experience brought home one lesson very sharply – the future existence must be consistent with safety, hygiene and sustainable way of operations in every sphere. The top echelons of the industry have always played a pioneering role in innovative sustainable practices and they continued with new initiatives during the year, matching the requirements of the situation. The year, however, witnessed acceptance of this need by all sections of the industry and spread of sustainability awareness among SMEs and establishments in two to three tier cities. The Hotel Association of India led the way through consistent advocacy through its magazine, Engage, and its newsletters and with national and global collaborations with organisations like WTTC Sustainability Basic and UNICEF.

Domestic travel played an important role in shaping the industry in 2022. Domestic tourism has always been the most prominent feature of growth of Indian tourism and hospitality, but its integral importance for the survival and growth of the sector was perhaps never as much realised as in 2022. The year is marked by empowerment of the consumers'—changes in the preferences of travellers. New expressions like "staycation" and "bleisure" have become part of the travel vocabulary and the hotels have to adjust to the changes with flexible reservation and cancellation policies. Across the industry, travellers' preference for leisure travel was noticeable and places like Goa, Kashmir, Himachal Pradesh and Uttarakhand attracted high number of travellers throughout 2022.

Predominance of the use of technology and digitisation of many of the operations for customer relations and servicing marked the revival of the industry. At the same time, globally as well as in India, staff shortages caused serious concern. In Europe and elsewhere, post-Covid-19 experience of labour shortage, caused by people who moved due to closure or decline of business or for better options was a disturbing factor. Hospitality giant Accor, for example, reported a loss of about 15 percent labour. The civil aviation services in Europe reported severe impact of labour shortage. Some tremors were felt in India as well and the wider question of manpower management would be a matter for attention in 2023.

The year 2023 holds even better promise but there are worries and uncertainties too. Occasional recurrence of the virus in different parts of the world, still uncertain behaviour of the monkey pox, the volatile global geo-political situation and looming threat of recession in major economies like USA should keep the industry on its toes. And topmost concern for the year should be not to relax on safety, hygiene and emphasis on sustainable practices.

The UNWTO Confidence Index surveys indicate that most experts see a potential return of international arrivals to 2019 levels in 2023. The tourism and hospitality industry will have to gear up for this growth in many ways - destination development, growth in civil aviation facilities to cater to the expected arrivals, proper marketing and confidence building measures to project a safe, sustainable experience, expansion of decent accommodation and so on.

The year 2023 is going to be an important one for India. As the President of G-20, India will host the summit, with more than 200 meetings across the country. G-20, with nearly 90 percent of the world's GDP, 80 percent of global trade and 67 percent of the world's population, exerts a significant political and economic influence. It will be a great opportunity to showcase and market the excellence of Indian tourism and hospitality. The G-20 summit will open new growth avenues for the Indian travel and hospitality ecosystem and bolster the demand for high-quality accommodation. The smooth running of these high - profile 200-plus meetings will support India's efforts to establish itself as a global MICE destination.

Preparing for the G-20 will be an opportunity to develop infrastructure – accommodation, civil aviation, destinations – for the growth of international tourist arrivals that the Ministry has projected. In that context it will be an appropriate occasion to give incentive in the form of "infrastructure status" which will increase investments that can bridge the gap in accommodation that the country faces. In 2023 if the Government usher in new initiative for PPP and stronger collaboration with the industry, many of the suggestions for taking Indian tourism and hospitality to the top, will see fruition.

During the period of survival, HAI had persistently asked for a pragmatic policy for liquidity support particularly for the SMEs as well as wage support for preventing job loss. Some other suggestions were:

- Rationalisation of taxes and tax rates, GST and a long-term interest rate structure;
- Policy Interventions for waiver of statutory dues etc for the period of closure of business;
- Easy compliances and ease of doing business, and incentives like ECLGS.

Many of those recommendations are still relevant even if the industry has been resilient enough to overcome the worst. Similarly providing "industry status" will spur growth of the sector and bring returns manifold for the economy.

23

WEATHERING THE STORM AND BUILDING ANEW[21]

Hospitality is central to Indian DNA and the tradition of treating guests like God still inspires the industry.

"The Hotel Association of India has been pleading for a constructive PPP to put this engine of growth in steam and for responsive and supportive policies, tax breaks, and moratoriums and so on to enable the industry to recover"

The year that just passed is best described, for the hospitality industry, as annus horribilis and best forgotten. As the beleaguered industry was picking up the threads to start the journey afresh, the fresh wave of the pandemic has again triggered uncertainty. Being hugely capital intensive, with high operating costs, the losses in the hotel industry have a multiplier effect. Every time there is a dip in travel sentiment the losses mount. The hotel industry has been cash strapped and burdened with increased costs of sanitisation, social distancing and other pandemic related SOPs. However, at the same time, the pandemic has reinforced the importance of not only physical immunity, but also mental well-being, increasing a craving for experiences beyond the mundane. There is an explosion in experiential categories, such as experiential retail, wellness holidays, and so on. As Covid-19 drives home the point of transience, people

21. BW Hotelier, 27 January, 2022.

are finding solace in small joys and meaningful encounters. That explains the rush of visitors to hotels, resorts right after the second wave. There are green shoots, and there is wisdom in looking at the positive side too, and in getting on to build back fast.

Luckily, Indian hospitality has always counted on offering extraordinary experiences, in terms of design, style, architecture, views, culture, and culinary varieties, that makes guest experience central to services. Even in remote corners of the country, where there may be little to offer beyond bed and breakfast, the guest is indulged with warm hospitality, exotic local cuisine and unrivalled local experiences that are unique to the place. Hospitality is central to Indian DNA and the tradition of treating guests like God still inspires the hospitality industry.

There could be a lull in the business outlook for at least for the next two fiscals, according to a report by Hotelivate, "Indian Hospitality-The Stats and Pulse Report". As per the report, the hotel occupancy is expected to breach the 65 percent threshold only by FY24, while pre-Covid-19 average daily rate (ADR) may be achieved by FY25. This assessment is in tune with the UNWTO's view that international tourist arrivals will come back to 2019 level only in 2024. Tourism revenue was down 72 percent over the previous year. The pace of recovery, according to UNWTO, remains slow and uneven across world regions due to varying degrees of mobility restrictions, vaccination rates and traveller confidence. "The economic contribution of tourism in 2021 (measured in tourism direct gross domestic product) is estimated at US$ 1.9 trillion (US$ 2.9 trillion), above the US$ 1.6 trillion in 2020, but still well below the pre-pandemic value of US$ 3.5 trillion," says UNWTO. The industry has to brace up for the ups and downs due to local restrictions, people's desire for social distancing, as well as sudden spurts in demand when the virus scare is lower.

The adversity taught some lessons too and most of those lessons will stay with the industry. It is certain that the huge disruptions caused by the pandemic will impact the hospitality sector. Several trends like that of automation, rapid technology adoption, contactless service delivery protocols, sustainability, hotel staff doubling as care ambassadors, and so on are there for all to see. Hotels have pivoted around servicing the prime needs of customers, that is, health, hygiene and safety.

While leading hotel brands have diversified offerings with cloud kitchens, and use of premises as quarantine centres, well thought-out curated experiences built around trust and safety will hold sway among people who would like to explore their innate desire to travel, albeit in a safe world. People who embark on a post pandemic journey will look for immersive experiences, possibly story telling around food, local crafts, traditional architectures, space history, like at old forts, and so on.

The trend towards personalisation will also make people look for greater ease and flexibility in booking and cancellations. Over 80 percent hotels today are either unbranded or standalone. It is these hotels that will have to do greater R&D to win the traveller back. The digital environment contains the largest catchment area of customers. Online presence, and increased automation is the reigning trend all through the industry - big hotels, or small.

It is known that the unprecedented storm has put the viability of a large portion of the industry at stake. Beyond the obvious, millions of jobs directly and indirectly as also the very process of economic recovery are at stake if this important pillar of inclusive growth is left tottering.

The Hotel Association of India has been pleading for a constructive PPP to put this engine of growth in steam and for responsive and supportive policies, tax breaks, and moratoriums and so on to enable the industry to recover. The industry on its side has to start a new, gathering the experiences of the last two years, keeping the long term view in mind, prioritising plans, investing time in building teams that are attuned and qualified to meet the new age challenges, keeping the focus on health and wellbeing of employees and guests. The industry is quickly adapting to new realities for business. Various studies have shown that more than 80 percent of key managers see digital transformation as the greatest change and challenge. Apart from enabling health and safety confidence in consumers, it helps in quick decision making, easier response to clients, increased efficiency, reduced cost and helps in survival by impacting the bottom line - revenue. WTTC reports that some European countries are facing a different problem - of staff shortages. In the immediate future, one area of opportunity will be the capacity to blend business with leisure and reorient the hotel facilities accordingly. Hospitality is a service industry and new and unique experiences will be the greatest demand of future consumers. In that sense how to maintain a personal touch in a contactless era will continue to challenge the imagination and innovation of the industry.

24

COVID -19 UNDERSCORES NEED FOR DISASTER INSURANCE FUND FOR TOURISM[22]

"Tourism touches everyone" is the slogan the Ministry of Tourism had carried to demonstrate the wide impact of tourism on the economy. And therefore, the pain of the industry which has been totally halted like never before, spreads to millions beyond.

Any step towards recovery is a step to lessening the pain and stress that most of the industry is passing through because of no revenue and growing liabilities each passing day. The process of recovery should be seen as a step different from revival of the industry for which the government will have to attend to infrastructure development and confidence building measures.

The industry is heterogeneous, and the needs and the problems vary in content and magnitude. In India, as also the world over, SMEs comprise almost 80 percent of the industry that contributes 9 percent to India's GDP, employs nearly 4.5 crore people and provides livelihood to around 16 crore people. These SMEs are fighting a grim battle for survival. Millions of other service providers in the tourism industry who depend on such SMEs are also in dire straits.

They mostly need small support which are crucial for them--like innovative ways of payroll support during these months of 'no income, liquidity in general and working capital in particular, credit guarantee

22. Engage, Vol. 1, Issue 3, May-Jun 2021.

assistance, lower rate of interest for some time, deferment of taxes, licence fee etc due for payment now, moratorium on bank payments, review of the existing rules, procedures to see that they do not create stumbling blocks. Such measures will make the recovery process less painful and they are eminently doable in the larger interest of the economy. The Government of India's recovery programme is huge and happily largely directed towards the SME sector.

But the tourism industry felt hugely disappointed that their specific problems were not addressed. There is a strong case for looking at the problems of the tourism industry on a separate footing—unlike any other industry its basis is "peoples contact". Covid -19 has destroyed that very base and until immunity is found--and which is not likely to be soon-- the industry cannot hope for full recovery.

The Ministry of Tourism has been in dialogue with the industry to find out if the genuine problems of the industry are not being addressed and are trying to find solutions. This interaction should be systematised and seriously continued.

Even if the policies are right, problems will arise in interpretation and implementation. It will be good if the present system of MoT's response to industry could be formalised to create something like a Help Desk for one stop solution. Many of the problems are within the competence of the State Governments. Therefore, for quicker relief the state governments should be taken on board. It will be ideal if a coordination mechanism could be involved that includes MoT, state governments and the industry. For example, very rightly MoT has focused on domestic tourism to lead the revival. Quite rightly too SOPs have been issued to start hotels and restaurants keeping stringent health safety issues on top of the agenda. Yet, as the Hotel association of India has brought to the notice of MoT, most states have not responded and in others the parameters vary widely. Even if the implementation takes a little time depending on the spread of the virus, the task of preparation of the roadmap should be started now.

The relief measures should have ongoing assessment. For example the moratorium period was conceived some time back. It needs to be reviewed. Hotel Association of India in a White Paper submitted to the Governor of RBI has suggested that moratorium should be spread pragmatically. It requests short term restructuring to enable the industry to tide over the crisis. It points out that 50 percent of the INR 45,000 crore loan that the branded hotels have taken, face the risk of becoming NPA with all its attendant impact on the economy.

One of the grievances of the industry is that though tourism contributes so much to the economy directly or indirectly, it does not get the benefits of 'infrastructure' or 'industry'. For the long-term growth of the sector, this grievance should be very seriously examined.

Government is spending a huge amount of money for creating infrastructure and also for creating income and employment in the rural area, particularly under MNREGA. In the new tourism scenario of the future sustainable, responsible tourism is likely to play a big role and rural tourism will also become more in demand. It would be good to link, wherever relevant, some such expenditure to create domestic tourism infrastructure, destination refurbishing etc.

The future is very uncertain, and I can only repeat the famous quote that the only prediction that holds good is that no prediction will hold good. However, UNWTO has made a very striking comment that trust is the new currency. It is the trust in the destination's sustainability, capacity to assure health safety, hygiene and adherence to environmental and climate change concerns that will determine tourists' preferences. Covid -19 has made human beings look more closely at the might of nature and at the importance of being responsible. Tourists are likely to be more discerning and demand commitment to the norms of Sustainable Development.

The Responsible Tourism Society of India and the MoT have some understanding to put in place the criteria for responsible tourism and how to make that a part of existence of all tourism service providers in India. Responsible tourism involves tourists, the host community, the service providers and the government. Responsible tourism may no longer be an option—it will be a necessity.

Four 'I's are likely to play a game changing role in the future—artificial Intelligence, IT, Ideas and Innovation. The competitive edge will be determined by the industry's capacity to respond to new situations with new solutions quickly.

The industry, to be in tune with these new norms, will need to make proper investment. They will also have to take up proper skilling programmes. But, the industry so badly torn by Covid-19, may not be in a position to venture into such investments. Government should therefore facilitate this transition by innovative public-private partnership measures.

A crisis of this magnitude cannot be normally anticipated. We had small tremors earlier from tsunami and SARS and should have thought about some disaster management policy. The general NDMA for the country as a whole, provides holistic planning. But tourism problems being so different, there should be a Tourism Disaster Management Body—preferably within NDMA. This body should prepare mitigation strategy modules under different possible scenarios which can be put into operation whenever a disaster strikes. For example, there should be some templates for relief like deferment of taxes etc, moratorium and those should immediately be applicable under the norms already decided upon.

Covid-19 experiences have also underscored the need for some sort of disaster insurance fund. This fund can be created as a model Public Private Partnership by initial corpus from government and suitable recurring deposits. Members of the industry who wish to be part of it contribute say 0.05 percent of the annual profit. A fund so created, can help the members in times of crisis involving disruption of business by way of say salary support, bank guarantee support etc. The modalities can be worked out.

Overall, we need to take a holistic view. The model of global recovery plan mooted by UNWTO revolves around the theme of Responsible Tourism Recovery—for people, for the planet and for prosperity—with social inclusion, public health and good governance as the prime movers.

The New Future

25

POST PANDEMIC TOURISM—SUSTAINABILITY IS THE KEY[23]

With the increasing number of tourists, there has been tremendous pressure on the natural ecosystems, especially at popular destinations.

With the increasing number of tourists, there has been tremendous pressure on the ecosystems, especially at popular destinations.

Before the pandemic brought tourism to a standstill globally, Indian tourism had seen a period of robust growth. India ranked 22nd in International Tourist Arrivals—a remarkable achievement from a rank of 43 only a decade back. Tourism is the largest service industry in the country that contributes to 6.8 percent of GDP (2019). The impact of tourism in creating income and employment and in contributing to inclusive growth is far reaching and is well established.

However, with the increasing number of tourists, there has been tremendous pressure on the natural ecosystems, especially at popular destinations. Be it depletion of groundwater levels, increase in vehicular pollution or waste generation, various tourist destinations across the country are facing a severe ecological crisis. The pandemic has brought the sustainability issues to the forefront and in future tourists' choices are likely to be more dependent on

23. ET Hospitality World, April 29, 2021.

how a destination addresses such concerns. It is now the correct time to plan for post-covid tourism recovery. Therefore, it is the time to look at the need for providing not only luxurious, safe and authentic experiences to tourists but also protecting the social, cultural and environmental integrity of destinations.

Paraphrasing the time-honoured definition of sustainable development, it can be said that sustainable tourism is the form of tourism that meets the needs of tourists, the tourism industry, and host communities, today without compromising the ability of future generations to meet their own needs. Such tourism is economically viable but does not destroy the resources on which the future of tourism depends, notably the physical environment and the social fabric of the host community. UNWTO has defined the Triple Bottom Line of sustainable action as economic efficiency and self-reliance, environmental and economical harmony, and social equity, empowerment and capacity building.

The domestic tourism visits before the pandemic was estimated to be a staggering 1800 million. As soon as the covid situation eases, the pent-up demand is likely find avenues to satisfy the urge to travel. There will be a long list of things to be done to make the recovery smooth, safe and tension free. We can mention three things that should receive priority attention.

First, overriding everything else is the concern for saving lives, the importance of strictly following the SOPs by all the stakeholders. This will require a strong PPP initiative. Second, the pandemic has significantly changed the tourist attitudes. The customer's choice is likely to be for short, safe road journeys and destinations that inspire confidence about health safety. Creation of new destinations and creating new experiences, their professional management, involving the local community should be at the top of the agenda of the government. Fortunately, the draft National Tourism Policy has treated it as a priority area. Third, it is necessary to evolve a code of ethics for sustainable behaviour making the government, the tourists, the private sector and the local community partners in creating a responsible tourism environment in the country.

India has been alive to the requirements of sustainable tourism, though the sense of responsibility has not taken deep roots yet. In August 2014, Ministry of Tourism had launched the Comprehensive Sustainable Tourism Criteria for India (STCI) for Accommodation, Tour Operators and Beaches, Backwaters, Lakes and Rivers sectors. Many destinations have shown the lead. Such initiatives link tourism successfully to the local community creating a model for empowerment and development of the people in the area while sustaining eco-friendly tourism. This is achieved through a three-pronged strategy encompassing economic, social and environmental responsibility.

The pandemic offers an opportunity to tread off the beaten track to make sustainable tourism an engine for economic growth. Consumer preferences and tourism policies the world over are expected to evolve towards achieving greater sustainability and community orientation. We are likely to see a trend towards taking cognizance of environmental costs beyond economic costs; destinations that will move towards a zero-carbon footprint along with higher levels of hygiene; tour operators and hoteliers gravitating towards more responsible and meaningful experiences; showcasing the local for the global; and positioning the host community as the centrepiece of the tourist experience.

Long term sustainability requires a balance between sustainability in economic, sociocultural, and environmental terms. The need to reconcile economic growth and sustainable development also brings in an ethical dimension. Tourism will thus emerge as a key factor in eco-development in the coming years and can only develop with people's participation. It is more important than ever that we support green innovation as a catalyst of tourism's sustainable growth.

26

ADAPTING TO CHANGE: HOSPITALITY EDUCATION IN POST COVID ERA[24]

Digital transformation is a very broad concept but simply put it will imply more use of Information and Communication Technology in hospitality.

Digital transformation is a very broad concept but simply put it will imply more use of Information and Communication Technology in hospitality.

The pandemic has impacted business across the world like never before in recent memory. There are no definitive estimates as yet of the total impact, but various assessments like that of RBI, the UNWTO, McKinsey and a recent report of EXIM Bank show the Indian hospitality sector as one of the worst hit by the first and second wave of covid-19. While the biggest challenge before the industry is survival, it has also to be alive to many opportunities likely to come up in the changed new normal situation. As is often said, disruptive experiences lead to innovations. The future of the industry will be influenced greatly by innovative practices and the hospitality education system will have to adapt, adjust and innovate to be in tune with this new demand.

---

24. ET Hospitality World, Jun 2, 2021.

The tourism and hospitality industry is almost unanimous in the opinion that digital transformation is both the challenge and the opportunity of the future. Digital transformation is a very broad concept but simply put it will imply more use of Information and Communication Technology.

Need to adapt to change

Technology is the most enabling change to which the industry has to adapt. Technology is used to serve a purpose. It serves the specific goals of each enterprise using it. And these goals are not uniform. The efficacy of the technology used in an organisation depends on the men using the technology. And education plays the key role in orienting the human resources to use technology to advantage. Market dynamics are changing fast. Enterprises would primarily like to use technology to reduce cost, free up time and resources, help customers connect and respond quickly to their needs.

Hospitality education in India faces the critical question- if digitalisation and innovation are the future realities, are they equipped now or expect to be in the future, to be in tune with this change? Hospitality education in the future will have to embrace two broad dimensions. First, to provide orientation and enable human intervention to use and adapt technology to the specific requirements of each enterprise. Second, technology is fast changing. And often technology can become obsolete even before it is fully assimilated to the system. The good manager has to be in continuous training mode and the educational institutions must be capable of providing that "continuous mode". The institutions will have to be always abreast of change in curriculum, teaching methods, quality of teachers to remain relevant. It will put a huge strain on the traditional mode of hospitality education in terms of qualified teachers and financial capability to move with change.

Developments in Hospitality Education

Covid has changed the mode of imparting education. It is now education without school. There are many questions still to be answered. Is it going to be the norm rather than exception? Can it meet the full range of the broad objectives of learning, including personal improvement?

Hospitality educational institutions have been reacting to the crisis since the beginning of 2020. More and more of them are now anticipating the demands of their existing and future students and mobilising their resources in a timely manner to respond to those needs. The switch from physical learning to distance learning requires an adaptation in the content and curriculum, but even more in terms of students' hands-on experience.

Can the virtual reality experience replace essential practical teaching? If remote learning is going to be the norm students must have a sense of belonging and the right support from their school. Career support like bespoke career counselling, online interview techniques, career workshops, and access to career opportunities must also be included. Distance learning can be challenging and disengaging; therefore, institutions can offer remote students one-to-one online mentoring sessions with programme leaders and faculty to bring a personal touch to distance learning and keep them motivated. The education system is shifting towards more self-learning, e-learning and tools that can adapt to the capability of each student. Learning can happen on multiple devices - the theory online and the practice taking place physically. There are a lot of grey areas about the future and it is time to discuss and debate the various options.

Here's what the future looks like!

UNWTO has surveyed and summed up some emerging trends. Travelling is more of an experience off the beaten track rather than just a visit. Second, they look for open air, hygienic accommodation, nature and rural ambience. Travellers look for local cuisine, craft, art and culture as part of their experience. Concern for sustainability is stronger than ever before. And above all tourism is not an end in itself-it is a means. People matter and therefore tourism is best when it is community centric.

Tourism education has a role to play in responding to these trends. Experience economy makes each tourist a market. The service must match and therefore multi-skilling is an integral part of training. Authentic storytelling is an essential part of the visitor experience. HRD can create not only good guides but also good managers who are storytellers.

But all the organised education facilities come to just a drop in the ocean. Large section of hospitality, hotels, restaurants, resorts, homestays - are outside the training circle. If the quality of service is to meet the new norms, the scope of human resource development will have to be expanded to cover larger service providers. That is possible only by adopting a pragmatic "training of trainers" programme as part of a dynamic PPP.

The Pandemic has taught many lessons. Sustainability is not just a slogan but a survival mantra for humanity. Each of us has a responsibility to others, to society, to the ecosystem and to the only planet we have. Difficult though it is, the education system has the task of creating human resources capable of managing AI and innovations but also emotionally attuned to the needs of a future sustainable and responsible tourism and hospitable industry.

27

TOURISM RISES TO CLIMATE CHANGE CHALLENGE[25]

There is much scope to look at fuel efficient technology and techniques.

As the world awaits once again with great expectation for the outcome of the COP 26 conference in Glasgow in 2021 and the emergence of another set of global action to meet the challenges of climate change, travel and tourism industry has declared its resolve to unitedly meet its climate action responsibilities. Continuing its commitment of G-20 Tourism meet in Rome for "one planet tourism" Glasgow declaration, piloted by World Tourism Organisation (UNWTO), and joined by the UN Environment Programme (UNEP), United Nations Framework Convention on Climate Change (UNFCCC) and others, is a commitment "to deliver plans aligned with these pathways to cut tourism emissions in half over the next decade and reach Net Zero emissions as soon as possible before 2050".

The gap between intent and action - as Eliot would say "between the idea and the reality, falls the shadow" has been a major tragedy of global action. Nevertheless, the resolve of the tourism industry comes as a fresh wind as the run up to the COP 26 has not seen many instances to cheer.

25. ET Hospitality World, Nov 8, 2021.

UN's Intergovernmental Panel on Climate Change (IPCC) recent report was termed "code red for humanity" by the UN Chief. The report highlights how climate change is taking its toll and how global action targets appear tenuous. In a sense it also shows where hope lies. For example, it says human influence is "very likely" (90%) the main driver of the global retreat of glaciers since the 1990s and the decrease in Arctic sea-ice. If it is primarily a result of human action, human resolve can also turn the tide. Since 1970, global surface temperatures have risen faster than in any other 50-year period over the past 2,000 years. It is not surprising that not too long back scientific study was seriously looking at the possibility of going back to the ice age. Newsweek in 1975 wrote "the earth's climate seems to be cooling down". Even in 1976 National Geographic, Time magazine were debating if it was cooling off or warming.

Unfortunately, the history of global action to meet the challenge does not make a happy reading, Rio 92, Johannesburg World Summit 2000, Millennium Development Goals, Sustainable Development Goals, Paris Agreement-all achieved targets only halfway. Perhaps the world was in denial, requiring the then SG of UN, Ba Ki Moon to exclaim "it is real, it is fast increasing and it affects us all". Actor Robert Redgrave, UN Brand Ambassador for Climate Change had said that time for half measures and climate denial was over. Just before the Glasgow conference the UN Framework Convention on Climate Change said that the world was on "catastrophic pathway" to 2.7 degree warming. The 2020 global average temperature at 1.2 degree above preindustrial baseline is considered to be woefully off track to stay below 1.5 degree as per Paris Agreement. As recently as on 17th September the UN Secretary General was reported to have said that the Paris Agreement could go up in smoke.

Against such a background, the Glasgow Declaration of tourism may look like a pious hope. Nevertheless, it is time that the industry rises to the challenge. There is evidence to show that tourism action can help substantially. During 2020 when travel had stopped, global carbon dioxide emission fell by 6.4 percent--approximately 2.3 billion tonnes. A study by UNWTO has established the responsibility of the travel and tourism sector. It shows that by 2030 transport-related CO^2 emissions from tourism will grow 25 percent from 2016 levels (from 1597 Mt of CO^2 to 1998 Mt of CO^2). This growth in CO^2 emissions will represent 5.3 percent of all man-made emissions in 2030 (from 5 percent in 2016). Transport-related emissions from domestic tourism are expected to grow by 21 percent from 2016 to 2030 (from 913 Mt CO^2 to 1103 Mt CO^2). Transport-related CO^2 emissions of the tourism sector are 22 percent of the whole emissions.

Tourism climate action plans to achieve the objectives through five pathways of action-

- measure all the tourism related emissions by everyone and share data, information;
- then take action to decarbonise in all tourism activities;
- regulate and restore the ecosystems;
- collaborate among the stakeholders and
- lastly, provide finance to implement the action plans.

It is significant that the 'pathways' indicate responsibilities for all the stakeholders including the local communities and visitors. In spirit and intent at least, it attempts to recover the soul of Rio Local Agenda 21 recognising that without shared responsibilities at the local level, any plan would be effectively rootless.

A TERI report had shown that India loses 6 percent of GDP due to environmental related deficiencies. Enterprises are intrinsic to sustainable solutions. Indian hospitality industry has shown awareness of the challenge as well as the responsibilities. Sustainable practices are part of many initiatives and innovations of big hotels like Taj, Oberoi, ITC, Radisson etc. ITC had shown how use of solar power can save 15 litres of diesel per hour. Chalet group had recently pledged to move to 100 percent renewable electricity by 2031 and 100 percent electric vehicle fleet by 2025.

These are just some examples of possible action by the sector but all such action at present touch only the tip of the iceberg. Looking at the growing mass of alarming evidence about the threatening advance of climate change and the positive role that the hospitality sector can play, it can be said that the response will have to be much more intensive as well as extensive. The aviation sector, another key player has committed to meet the Paris Agreement targets but actual action seems to be far behind. UN's Environmental Programme said that government fossil fuel production plan for the decade was "dangerously out of sync" with the emissions cut needed. Another UN report has said that various countries are planning to produce more than double the amount of fossil fuel than is consistent with limiting global warming to 1.5 degrees. Indian aviation had heralded the use of biofuel. It is time to go from that beginning to exploring many more possible options of wider use of biofuels. There is much scope to look at fuel efficient technology and techniques.

There is much more at stake in COP 26 than just capacity to draw up targets and action plans. If Corona-19 has taught any lesson, it is that the future of human existence is at stake. What Benjamin Franklin had said in a different context is so pertinent today - "we must indeed all hang together, or most assuredly we shall all hang separately".

28

HOSPITALITY INDUSTRY—COMMITTED TO THE PLANET AND PROSPERITY[26]

While climate change hopefully will engage more specific action as it should, beyond grandiose conferences and pious declarations, the focus on the wider problems of sustainability must not be lost sight of.

As the headlines scream of “Heat Apocalypse” and Europe burns with unprecedented heat wave and uncontrolled forest fires, as Europe’s mightiest river and tourism showpiece Rhine dries up, scientists blame climate change, the words of the then UN Secretary General, Ba Ki Moon rings loud. “Climate Change” he had warned “is real, it is accelerating, and it threatens all of us”. He pointed out three gaps in the climate change strategy-that the reality has not dawned on the common people, that it is not seen as an individual problem and that it is catching on us fast.

While climate change hopefully will engage more specific action as it should, beyond grandiose conferences and pious declarations, the focus on the wider problems of sustainability must not be lost sight of. Climate change action requires united effort to undo the

26. ET Hospitality World, Aug 10, 2022.

follies of mankind. Sustainability needs more. The devastating pandemic-Covid-19 has shown that the world needs positive action involving everyone to adopt a sustainable way of life to rebuild the only planet we have.

In fact, much before Covid-19, the SDG objectives had outlined strong role for sustainable tourism action. While goals 8, 12 and 14 directly related to tourism, UNWTO had maintained that tourism was directly or indirectly related to all the goals. The nature of tourism is such that it affects everyone, and the ripple effects go through all layers of the economy and society. During the pandemic, the TBILISI declaration of 2020 projected a design for future tourism as one for the people, for the planet and for prosperity, identifying the possible contributions of tourism to sustainable and inclusive growth.

In the aftermath of Covid-19 the UNWTO had outlined various trends that were likely to shape tourism and hospitality sector of the future. Sustainability emerged as the most dominant and unanimous future concern. It was forecast that we were likely to see a trend towards taking cognisance of environmental costs beyond economic costs; destinations that will move towards a zero-carbon footprint along with higher levels of hygiene; tour operators and hoteliers gravitating towards more responsible and meaningful experiences; showcasing the local for the global; and positioning the host community as the centrepiece of the tourist experience.

These trends are visible now. Millennials and Gen Z is now moving towards the change. According to a recent report by Booking.com 91 percent of Indian travellers want to travel sustainably in the coming months. In addition to that, while 94 percent of travellers confirmed that sustainable travel is important to them, 68 percent cited recent news reports about climate change that influenced their choices.

Successful development of sustainable tourism can evolve only with the shared responsibility of all the stakeholders—the government, the travellers, the service providers like hotels, tour operators and the host community. In August 2014, Ministry of Tourism had launched the Comprehensive Sustainable Tourism

Criteria for India (STCI) for Accommodation, Tour Operators and Beaches, Backwaters, Lakes and Rivers sectors.

Fortunately, despite being ravaged by the pandemic the hospitality industry has shown great responsibility in responding to the challenges. Hotel chains and accommodation places have started taking steps for responsible tourism while carving out the future of Indian hospitality. Some of the initiatives are visible in creating a sustainable experience for the customers—like use of organic materials, limiting the use of plastic, picking ecologically-friendly solutions like investing in green energy, preserving biodiversity, leading campaigns and initiatives to keep beaches, hill resorts clean, water saving filters, waste reductions, use of electric cars and solar panels. Also noticeable is the increasing use of CSR to, champion the cause of cleanliness and indigenising campaigns, promote local handicrafts, culture and skills to expand livelihood opportunities to local communities. Technology has been used by the industry to promote sustainable practices increasingly.

Such initiatives are in tune with the TBLISI declaration. Hotel Association of India takes justifiable pride in showcasing the initiatives of its members on most of the above issues and making hospitality through its sustainable supply chain a tool for inclusive growth. HAI's support for the global initiative 'Hotel Sustainability Basics' of World Travel and Tourism Council (WTTC) to promote responsible tourism also provides a good opportunity to the hospitality fraternity to take visible steps for sustainability.

Considering the enormity of the challenges these are certainly small steps. But if all small things add together to create a movement and inspire everyone, much would have been achieved. There is much to be done by all. Most of the present initiatives are largely confined to the bigger hotel chains and should percolate down. Government's 2014 initiative should be reviewed in the light of recent experiences and a more comprehensive, responsible initiatives which encourage, motivate and compel all stakeholders to move towards the common objective, should be developed. The small and medium enterprises which is the biggest component of the sector, will need motivation, incentives and support in developing and adopting new technology and methods. And above all it requires total involvement of the local communities, their acceptance of the sustainable practices and their willingness to demand for the same. It also requires continuous research to develop green practices which are not only viable but also profitable and the industry should be incentivised to replicate them.

All that is possible if there is strong determination of the government and a robust system of PPP for taking all the stakeholders along.

29

RETHINKING TOURISM[27]

Ever since WTO started keeping data on tourist arrivals in the last decades of the last century, tourism has grown continuously, aways outpacing the world economic growth. The pandemic brought that crashing down.

As the tourism industry slowly comes out of the worst crisis in its history, learning many lessons from the Covid-19 pandemic, it is only appropriate to pause and introspect on the World Tourism Day for 2022 on the theme - "Rethinking Tourism". The grim experiences during the pandemic brought home quite a few lessons and as the process of recovery starts, it is the time to reflect on the journey ahead. Rethinking is necessary on a wide range of issues but on top of the agenda is the necessity of recognising tourism as a crucial pillar of development and progress. And that is what the UN discussed in a special debate in May 2022- the first time that tourism was the subject of a special discussion.

World Tourism Organisation (WTO), subsequently UNWTO has been celebrating World Tourism Day since 1980 often on specific micro concerns of the industry. This year's theme is generic-reflecting concern for growth of tourism as a whole. Ever since WTO started keeping data on tourist arrivals in the last decades of the last century, tourism has grown continuously, aways outpacing the world economic

---

27. ET Hospitality World, Sep 27, 2022.

growth. At the beginning of the new century, 9/11 was a big jolt- and for the first time there was a dip in tourism growth. SARS, Tsunami, and the financial crisis soon followed affecting tourism but as always tourism bounced back and the projected 1.4 billion tourist arrivals by 2020 was achieved two years ahead of forecast.

In this journey the celebrations were in numbers. The pandemic brought that crashing down. International tourism went back to the levels of what was 30 years ago putting at stake 100-120 mn direct jobs, loss of up to USD 1.2 trillion in international visitors spending and loss of USD 2 trillion of global GDP.

The rethinking is envisioned to put people and planet first, bring all the stakeholders-government, business and communities together in making tourism more sustainable, inclusive, responsible and resilient and emphasising that tourism is a means to a better quality of life for all people, and not an end in itself of number crunching.

In fact, the warning bells were sounded long back in 1987 in that landmark report "Our Common Future". Five years later the leaders of the world met in Earth Summit in Rio to chalk out a sustainable path for the future of humanity. Twenty years later a review of Rio Agenda 21 led to another call for a "Future We Want". It required the pandemic to bring home the realisation that future is here and now but not the way we want. UNWTO says Covid-19 "is a watershed moment to align the effort of sustaining livelihoods dependent on tourism to SDG and ensure a more resilient, inclusive, carbon neutral and resource efficient future".

Beyond the broader issues and ideas that the Tourism Day theme evokes, for India it is a day to begin introspection on a number of issues like better management of impact of tourism, diversifying and spreading the benefits of tourism, managing destinations away from the cities, involving the local communities, harnessing the power of technology and creating capacity and putting tourism in its due place in national economic planning. Prime Minister Modi has often described tourism as a pillar of development. But it is not reflected in the policies and practices of the government.

The underlying spirit of RIO's Local Agenda 21 of starting the process from the grass roots, of involving the communities in matters that affect their future, should be built into the tourism policy and strategy.

While the tourism@47 vision of a US$ 1 trillion tourism economy and US$ 250 billion contribution to GDP, creating 53 million jobs by 2028 should make tourism a great catalyst for economic growth, much attention needs to be given to avoiding the negative impact of tourism. In a tourism world described as "experience economy", tourists will place more value on the experiences than on brand publicity. However, if tourism is to become an effective instrument of inclusive growth across the country, it will require strategical intervention to geographically diversify the tourism product and tourist arrivals. The distribution of tourists, domestic and international, is rather skewed so far. The top ten states/UTs get 87.2 percent of foreign tourists and 7 percent of domestic visits. The other 26 states/UTs receive on an average 0.5 percent of arrivals.

The rethinking is incomplete without an assessment of the overarching impact of fast changing technology. As the UNCTAD Technology and Innovation Report 2021 points out, the pace of change seems likely to accelerate as a result of "frontier technologies" such as artificial intelligence (AI), robotics, biotechnology, and nanotechnology. Technology empowers. But the pace of change, with each new development compounding the speed and reach of everything that came before, creates problems of adoption and adaptation. While it opens the doors of opportunity, dynamic skilling policies should create capacity to go through those doors. In absence of such a strategy there is apprehension of a digital divide of "haves" and "have nots" creeping in.

Similarly, climate change will transform tourism destinations, demand patterns, and investment for decades to come. We have to be part of a new era of climate resilient tourism. Globally Tourism has been estimated to contributes some 8 percent to global emissions. Tourism industry is increasingly committing to a net-zero target for 2050 and our commitment should also be apparent and effective.

30

WINDOW OF OPPORTUNITY FOR TOURISM[28]

The most important question to be addressed for quick implementation of the vision for tourism is getting the convergence of all the stake-holders.

"Tourism on a roll"- flashed the headlines after the last budget announcements where tourism got prominent mention. One is reminded of the classic lines from Dickens's novel- "It was the best of times; it was the worst of times." Only two years back the industry had experienced unprecedented devastation and was facing a bleak uncertain future.

Suddenly 2023 seem to have changed it all. The recovery news has been astounding, pushing to background the despair and despondency of the preceding years. Horwath HTL (HHTL), a leading global hospitality consultant, in its year-end report called 2022 a dream year for the Indian hospitality industry. 65 percent of respondents to a survey conducted by them say it was their best year ever; another 30 percent ranked it as among the three best years ever for their hotel. UNWTO had predicted during the worst crisis that the seeking, roving spirit of humans will ensure that tourism will bounce back. But the quick recovery is also a great testimonial to the resilience and entrepreneurship of the industry.

28. ET Hospitality World, Mar 28, 2023.

However, more significant than the AVRs, occupancy rates and tourist arrival numbers is the wind of change that is blowing. For the first time in recent memory the Finance Minister included a policy perspective for tourism in the budget speech. UNWTO has urged that it is time to transform potential of tourism to prosperity. Hotel Association of India has consistently advocated that such transformation is possible if tourism is made an input in the total economic development planning of the country. The sum total of the budget announcements on tourism in fact amount to accepting that role.

FM's reference was not a passing one. It is a brief, compact, comprehensive articulation of a vision and it is worth recapitulating. The central idea is to development tourism in a "mission" mode. It implies setting a definite goal, creating constructive partnership with the private sector, convergence of all the stakeholders, people's participation, professional development of destinations keeping the sustainability goals in view.

Again, in a refreshing departure from the routine, the way forward for this vision was discussed in a series of webinars and PM by addressing the webinar highlighted the importance attached by the government. PM's pragmatic suggestions painted the outlines of what a "mission" approach should be. It requires a goal-in case of tourism it is inclusive growth that it serves best. It has to be a long-term plan with innovative, imaginative "out of the box" thinking, sustainable, putting more emphasis on quality rather than quantity. The essence of PM's message was his reference to implementation.

The post-budget webinar was a good attempt to start the process of collaborative thinking. It did produce a huge number of suggestions and many "wish lists". That is understandable as the possibilities and potential are immense and much remains to be done. It will be necessary for MOT to separate the wheat from the chaff, and to focus on what the PM called long term planning that sets the short- and long-term priorities clearly.

The most important question to be addressed for quick implementation of the vision for tourism is to get the convergence of all the stake-holders of centre and states, of public and private sector, of 37 ministries in the centre that play a role in making professional tourism possible and similar convergence within the state departments.

As the PM said, this newfound optimism is also a time for 'out of the box' thinking. A professional, mission approach to tourism also needs some fundamental institutional changes. The concept of a National Tourism Board, which was recommended by the National Committee on Tourism in 1988 and which has been mooted by MOT recently, should be seriously examined and implemented without delay. Such a Board will facilitate involvement of the private sector and allow professional, accountable management of tourism development. As tourism is not in the Concurrent List, the essential convergence between the centre and the states as also between the different ministries of the central government is best achieved by creating a powerful institution like a National Tourism Council or Authority, preferably chaired by the PM. As is often said, opportunities are like sunrises. If you wait too long, you miss them. It is now the time to seize the golden opportunity that tourism has got and to transform the vision into a reality.

31

TOURISM VISION FOR INDIA @2047[29]

The upcoming years' vision must be dynamic to the ever-changing requirements of the sector. And, must be focused on quality and execution as well.

Twenty-five years is not a long time in the life of a nation. But things change. One remembers the words of Arthur C Clarke towards the end of the last century "the future is not what it used to be". It was also the time when Charles Handy famously wrote in his books that we were entering an "Age of Unreason" where the world was experiencing changes at such rapid pace that no future projection or prediction holds true. As is often said, "technology developing at an ever-accelerating rate of speed with each new technology compounding the speed and capabilities of those that came before" has certainly made the future different from what it used to be.

In such a volatile and dynamic world, a static future vision will be an anachronism. While the vision should be firm, its supporting action should be open to constant review and flexibility to respond to emerging changes.

The draft National Tourism Policy has been on the anvil for a while. It gives an indication of the directions in which the government would like to move in the journey to 2047. The vision in the draft

29. Engage, HAI. Vol. 2, Issue 4. Jul-Aug, 2022.

is “to transform our tourist destinations to provide world-class visitor experience making India one of the topmost destinations for sustainable and responsible tourism.” The vision of making India a top destination is unexceptionable. However, it becomes problematic if measured in terms of numbers. The goal of the policy indicates such an inclination. The overall goal of the Policy is “to make India one of the top 5 destinations in the world in terms of both, the international arrivals and international tourism receipts by 2030.”

The top destinations receive upwards of 50 million tourists against current arrivals to India of around 10 million. The fivefold jump in 8 years is ambitious, though possible. But the other destinations will also move upwards in the meantime and the target will shift. In the National Action Plan of 1992, it was envisaged that the share of foreign tourist arrival, which was only 0.04 percent, will grow in five years to 1 percent. The arrivals did grow but as others were also growing, the 1 percent. target was reached only after 25 years. But more important questions remain. India has recorded huge domestic visits of more than 2200 million, and this number is certain to increase manifold with projected greater economic growth.

Such exponential growth will require commensurate growth in access by air, road and rail, last-mile connectivity, spread of destinations, expansion of decent accommodation, and so on. The Policy does identify the issues to be handled but it is not specific on the bigger question of “How”. It mentions the importance of following a whole new Government approach and a holistic framework for tourism development. This is necessary because most of those activities that translate the mission into effective action are not within the purview of the Ministry of Tourism. And an overriding question remains—can India manage such numbers sustainably?

This vision can be realised only if there is paradigm shift in approach to tourism development. The long road so far has been of disappointment and missed opportunities. The department of tourism was created only in the mid-1960s, over a decade after Independence. The first tourism policy was adopted two decades after that, in 1982. After Independence, the five-year plans were the indicators of government's economic thinking. For years, tourism was missing from such thinking. The first two five-year plans did not mention tourism nor provided funds for its development. The third, fourth, fifth and sixth plans mainly recognised the foreign exchange earning capacity of tourism and briefly touched on its employment and income generating potential. Only the seventh and eighth plans made refreshingly clear enunciation of the role and importance of tourism.

The financial allocations for the sector remained around 0.1 percent of the total all throughout. In 1988, the government constituted a National Committee on Tourism, which made some very far-reaching recommendations for development of tourism. Among others, it suggested—

(1) Restructuring the department and creating a National Tourism Board;

(2) A Standing Committee of Tourism Ministers for integrated approach;

(3) Tourism Planning to be integrated into the overall plans for the country.

All these recommendations have remained on paper only. They are still relevant and the introspection on tourism@2047 should include these issues also. In fact, the Prime Minister's oft quoted words that tourism is an important pillar of development, come close to affirming the third and the most important recommendation noted above.

It is relevant here to relate the experience of Mexico, narrated in his Indian National Tourism Day lecture by Mr. Antonio Savignac, one time Minister in Mexico and later Secretary General of UNWTO. In the 1960s, Mexico was looking at a growth model for the country. Their intensive search led to, he says, "one of the curious activities that continually kept appearing was the case of tourism....A strange beast that seemed to grow like a weed, with no fertiliser, irrigation care or attention." They realised the unique nature of tourism, which given its enormous variety of segments, can truly be developed anywhere, unlike agriculture, industry or mining. "To make a long story shorter, the Mexican government concluded that if tourism had grown so well and so consistently, with little if any, encouragement what would it not do with some help and support in planning, financing, promotion, facilitation and political and budgetary support".

This story can be the story of Indian tourism. The vision for 2047 will be a reality, all coordination would be achieved if the foundation of this "pillar" is firmly laid in the economic development planning structure of the country.

While such foundation can rightly get tourism its due as an input in development and inclusive growth, the lessons of Covid-19 and the emergent challenges make it necessary that the tourism vision for the future responds to such challenges. Sustainability is the biggest challenge before humanity. OECD in its 2021 report has pithily outlined a new approach: "To achieve sustainability, the tourism policy paradigm should shift from a growth-oriented model to an approach focused on the quality of this growth and its compatibility with the quality of life of residents."

When Covid-19 was raging, the Tbilisi declaration of UNWTO resolved to reconstruct tourism "for the People, for the planet and for Prosperity" by, among others "placing tourism, as a service trade, among the priorities for socio-economic recovery plans for its capacity to create jobs and transform societies with a strong multiplier effect on other sectors throughout its broad value chain".

Tourism's 25-year vision should herald the spirit of hundred years of Independence. But we should never lose sight of the profound truth in the words of Thomas Edison: "Vision without execution is hallucination."

32

CONVERGENCE—THE TIPPING POINT FOR TOURISM[30]

When so many players are involved, convergence, though much desirable, is also much difficult to achieve.

"It is significant that the MoT's Draft Tourism Policy identified 10 key stakeholders and 20 key ministries which had a role to play in total tourism development. In such a context, 'convergence' is a much more meaningful word expanding the horizon of 'cooperation'".

The future vision for tourism succinctly outlined by the Finance Minister in the 2023 budget may turn out to be the tipping point for Indian tourism. "Convergence" is the foundation of this vision. Way back in the 90s, there was a common refrain heard in the MoT that tourism is something everyone talked about, but no one cared. In my first book on Indian tourism while looking at the future, I had talked about the importance of "coordination" of activities of different players that make tourism possible. The background was an excellent study by WTTC pointing out that tourism either impacted on or was impacted by about 60 economic activities of which about 30 had more direct relationship. In common parlance, however, tourism was talked about only in terms of four or five of them like transport – air, road and sea, accommodation, destinations, shopping, guide and culture.

It is significant that the MoT's Draft Tourism Policy identified 10 key stakeholders and 20 key ministries which had a role to play in total

30. BW Hotelier, 19 April, 2023.

tourism development. In such a context, “convergence” is a much more meaningful word expanding the horizon of “cooperation”. It implies a positive alignment of understanding among all.

As the PM pointed out in the subsequent discussions, implementation strategy is of vital importance to transform the vision into a tipping point. Puneet Chhatwal, President, Hotel Association of India (HAI), has elaborated on the six ‘P’ strategy – Planning, Places, People, Policy, Process and Promotion – implicit in the vision as starting point for action.

The first step in implementation should be to put in place a mechanism for convergence at four levels

– between the 20 identified ministries in the Central Government,

– between the departments in the state governments,

– between the Centre and the states and

– between the government and the private sector.

Just to mention an example – Gati Shakti scheme can be the lifeline for future tourism growth. The project formulation checklist for Gati Shakti should also include one parameter i.e., the tourism importance of the project or its link to any tourism destinations. On the other hand, selection of new tourism destinations should be in sync with infrastructure being put in place by Gati Shakti.

When so many players are involved, convergence, though much desirable, is also much difficult to achieve. Like an orchestra, it needs a good conductor, an agency or institutional mechanism to set the engine in motion. Very appropriately, the Draft Tourism Policy 2021 has identified such mechanism both for the centre and for the states in the form of National Tourism Advisory Board, National Tourism Authority, Inter Departmental Coordination Committee - ideas endorsed wholeheartedly by the industry. The first mission in developing tourism in mission mode should be to transform these ideas into reality.

At the same time, the future vision must be supported by action on various related fields. For example, it is common sense that the

Ministry's objectives of 1 trillion tourism economy or 100 m tourist arrivals by 2047 may fall by the wayside unless they are synchronised with corresponding expansion of accommodation infrastructure. Creating accommodation is both time consuming and capital intensive. In that context, providing "infrastructure status" to the hospitality sector is so much of a logical corollary and makes so much of sound economic and common sense that Government's hesitation on the issue is totally unfathomable.

Providing such status will encourage investment capabilities within the Indian hospitality industry. That will be in tune with the Government's accent on atmanirbhar and will mobilise resources quickly and internally. Secondly, the resultant return to the economy in terms of employment and income, tax revenue generation will far outweigh the small cost of incentives. Third, it will prevent outflow of foreign exchange that any foreign investment entails.

A recent statement by the Minister of Tourism in the Parliament that the ministry endorses the idea of "industry" status to tourism and that 11 states have already announced the same, invited attention to another very important area of convergence – between the Centre and the states and between states. One remembers how during the early stages of recovery after the Covid pandemic, the domestic movements were hampered by multiplicity and conflicting processes and procedures across the states. Finance Minister emphasised the large potential to be tapped in tourism. Prime Minister spoke of "out of the box" solution. It is only appropriate that such approach should start with a close look at the "ease of doing business" in the sector, rationalised and harmonised throughout the country in tune with the "one India, one nation" approach.

"There is one thing stronger than all the armies in the world" wrote Victor Hugo, "and that is an idea whose time has come." There is elation on the expectation that the idea of tourism has arrived. It is also time for all the stakeholders to converge in action to ensure that "between the idea and the reality, between the motion and the act" shadows do not fall.

33

VISION FOR TOURISM AND HOSPITALITY[31]

Though the hospitality sector should have received a clearer attention in the Union budget, the vision for tourism in the budget is pragmatic, and the roadmap is well charted.

The expectations and excitement of another Union budget is now behind us. The build up to the budget and its aftermath followed the familiar pattern—the industry enthusiastically participated in the pre-budget discussions with the Finance Ministry, feeling happy that its suggestions seem to have received sympathetic attention. The aftermath was not much different. Hospitality industry felt that its expectations from the budget were not met. Small things which could have been accommodated with little or no financial implications, which could have spurred the industry to greater contribution to GDP, inclusive growth and job creation, did not receive attention.

Traditionally, the budget not only provides the picture of the finances of the country, it also lays down the directions of the macro-economic policies for larger economic objectives. Hotel Association of India (HAI) took care to make its suggestions not so much in terms of "asks" or "demands" but attuned them to the broad objectives of the government. They were grouped under policy intervention,

31. Engage, HAI, Vol. 3 Issue 1, Jan-Feb, 2023.

rationalisation of taxes and tax rates to achieve greater efficiency and productivity and changes that make compliances easy and doing business hassle-free. Though missing in details in the Budget these recommendations are expected to be addressed in the coming months as there is a mention of The Harmonised Master List of Infrastructure to be reviewed by an expert committee for recommending the classification and financing framework, about increased ease of doing business and other proposed reforms. The budget, with its focus on capital investment and infrastructure development, cannot in its implementation ignore the proposal for "infrastructure status" that will encourage "atmanirbhar" way of bridging the gap between demand and supply in tourism infrastructure. And for that matter, the objective of professional development of tourism in "mission mode" must be built on making tourism an "industry". It is necessary to accept the rationale of these suggestions and their relevance to the avowed objectives of growth of the tourism and hospitality sector.

The budget coincides with a strong revival of the hospitality sector and in that excitement there may be a danger of ignoring these long-term imperatives of growth for the sector. Emerging from perhaps the worst time ever, tourism and hospitality were pleasantly greeted by 2023 like a ray of fresh sunshine. The recovery has been astounding, pushing to background the despair and despondency of the preceding years. Horwath HTL (HHTL), a leading global hospitality consultant, in its year-end report called 2022 a dream year for the Indian hospitality industry. Nearly 65 percent of respondents to a survey conducted by them say it was their best year ever; another 30 percent ranked it as among the three best years ever for their hotel. The report highlighted Lack of Scale as a serious concern. The average size of new supply created in 170 hotels in 2022 was 65 rooms; 93 of these hotels had 50 rooms or less. Just two hotels had more than 300 rooms. On its own, the hospitality sector–the highest employment multiplier for every million rupees invested among all the sectors–has a strong case for "big push" as infrastructure. And without it the mission mode of tourism will be limping on broken legs.

In fairness it must be said that the FM has painted the broad picture and the expectation is that the nitty- gritties will fall in place. Rarely has tourism found clear mention in the long term macro-economic directions of the country as it did in the current budget. In a few paragraphs, the FM has been able to pack a comprehensive, meaningful and futuristic vision for the sector, acknowledging the large potential to be tapped and the huge opportunities for job creation to be exploited. It is worthwhile paraphrasing the vision as enumerated as the guiding principles for the future. First is the need for a professional approach to tourism, a mission mode where the three key players converge—the states, different departments of government and the private sector. Quite often well-meaning initiatives of the MOT fall on the wayside for lack of convergence with the departments responsible for implementation of those programmes. The Mission mode is expected to remove these deficiencies.

Second, a recognition of the new trend in tourism - of creating experience. Destinations to be developed in an innovative manner as comprehensive packages where all elements like connectivity, physical and virtual, security, storytelling, culture and cuisine are integrated. The experience of tourists will be enhanced by development of theme-based circuits. Significantly, it clearly brings out the importance of domestic tourism development as the foundation for the future tourism vision.

During the pandemic, the UNWTO had made an important TBILISH Declaration on the theme of the People and the Planet as the future focus and had carried it forward subsequently in the World Tourism Day theme of Rethinking Tourism. The Vision outlined by the FM rests on sustainable concerns—bio-diversity, carbon stock, ecotourism—where the local communities are at the centre and participate in the development and derive economic benefits from such participation.

A survey by UNWTO had found that for about 30 percent of travellers, shopping is a primary motivation during travel. India is a shopper's paradise in terms of the variety of arts and crafts. However, quite often travellers complain about hassles in shopping and about price and quality. It will be interesting to see if the concept of Unity Mall and development of local handicrafts and crafts transform the shopping experience of travellers and create avenues for income and employment for local artisans through tourism.

Last, by no means least, it is heartening to see the FM highlight the importance of skilling and entrepreneurship development in the sector. Tourism competitiveness revolves around the capacity to service experiences. And service now depends heavily on technology which is fast changing. To achieve the objective of seeing India as a top destination, attention to skilling will be an unavoidable requirement.

Overall, therefore the tourism and hospitality sector has much to be happy about the current budget. One is reminded of the famous quote in Alice in Wonderland-- “Would you tell me, please, which way I ought to go from here?” “That depends a good deal on where you want to get to,” said the Cat.

Though the hospitality sector should have received a clearer attention, the vision for tourism in the budget is pragmatic, and the roadmap is well charted. The hospitality sector will continue to hope that the rational suggestions of the sector will logically fall in place if the budget vision is properly and systematically implemented.

34

HOSPITALITY CATCHING TECHNOLOGICAL WAVES[32]

Adoption of new tech has become a tool for cutting-edge advantage in price war and shift in business strategies. The digital experience is however going much beyond automation.

In his futuristic book "Global Paradox", John Naisbitt narrates a story about technologies as the new god. "A theologian asked the most powerful supercomputer, 'Is there a God'? The computer said it lacked the processing power to know, asked to be connected to all the other supercomputers in the world. Still, it was not enough power. So, the computer was hooked up to all the mainframes in the world, and then all the minicomputers, and to all the personal computers. And eventually, it was connected to all the computers in cars, microwaves, VCRs, digital watches, and so on. The theologian asked for the final time 'Is there a God'? And the computer replied, 'There is Now!'

And that was in 1994!

Incredible things have happened since then. The evolution of civilisation has been marked by technological revolutions--like the steam engine, the printing press—all small as we look back, but

32. Engage, HAI, Vol. 2 Issue 3, May-June, 2022.

things that changed the world. The difference of the 21st century technological wave has been the sheer pace, "each new technology compounding the speed and capabilities of those that came before" and magnitude, the all-pervasive influence on human lives and activities. And this is only the beginning of the unknown frontiers. As the UNCTAD Technology and Innovation Report 2021 points out, the pace of change seems likely to accelerate as a result of "frontier technologies" such as artificial intelligence (AI), robotics, biotechnology, and nanotechnology. Fast pace of changes brings problems of adoption and adaptation. The Hospitality industry will have to continuously look for out-of-the-box responses to emerging challenges, competition and opportunities.

Starting with IT, going through CIT (Communication and Information Technology) and now digitisation is changing the world, and business. Richard Dobbs, James Manyika and Jonathan Woetzel, in the book "No Ordinary Disruption", tracing the global forces breaking the trends, point out how digitisation can affect business ideas. First, it converts physical goods into virtual. Second, it enhances the information content of many routine transactions—like RFID tags and 2-D bar codes. Third, "digitisation is creating online platforms that facilitate production and transaction and allow minnows to compete head-to-head with sharks". All these are eminently adoptable by the hospitality industry.

The post-pandemic world, including India, is facing a skills' gaps--shortages of skilled manpower. The story of skills gaps coexisting with high unemployment is not new. Dobbs et al. had pointed out in 2015 that by 2020 the world may have a gap of 85 million skilled and semi-skilled workers, alongside a surplus of 95 m low skilled workers. Lack of skilled workers can cause significant business problems of cost, quality and time. Smart use of technology, and coming out of the traditional mindset of using technology as a substitute to labour, can help the problem of skills gaps. First, research has shown that the use of technology can improve the productivity of existing skilled workers by 20 percent. Second, use of smart technology, along with training, can equip low-skill workers to perform high-skill jobs.

Experimentation with technology as a tool for business can be never-ending for the hospitality sector. For example, Dobbs has pointed out that the email was used as the first stage of digitisation by most businesses. It was soon experienced that using social platforms could improve knowledge workers' productivity by 20 percent. The story of Atos, a French IT services company, is often told. Eager to shift from the burden of email, which took 25 percent of employees' time, it shifted to the use of social community platforms. Within a week, it saw 20 percent reduction in email traffic.

Digitisation coinciding with the regime of "open data" has empowered both the consumer and the industry, each in its own way without conflict. Microsoft had boasted in 2015 that in the next five years they would generate more data than was generated in the previous 5000 years. And Microsoft is only one of the many players in data use. Technology empowers individuals and creates greater opportunities. It provides consumers with more choices vis-à-vis price, product, quality, service, and a host of other issues. That is reflected in greater demand for flexibility in bookings, cancellations, refunds, and so on. It also empowers the hospitality industry to upgrade marketing—to virtual reality, and online experiences.

During the peak of the pandemic, digitisation was used primarily for reducing physical interactions. It is no longer a short-term fix to overcome the pandemic problems. It has become a tool for cutting-edge advantage in price war and shift in business strategies. The digital experience is going much beyond automation. For example, (a) hotels can use digital technology to access data for proactive personalised marketing, (b) can make the new trend of staycation a reliable, innovative and enjoyable reality, (c) it can help in easy access to consumer database and its centralisation. An Amadeus study affirms that increasing digitalisation need not be in conflict with increasing personalisation–which is the strength of the hospitality business. With wider access to and use of expanding database at its disposal, combined with integrated technology, hotels can make customer experiences very personal and unique, (d) digitalisation is likely to be used more and more for shift from revenue management to profit management by allowing access to shared data across business "not just in silos". The strategic use of a wider range of data and integrated technology is expected to lead to proactive decision-making, increase efficiency in operations and reduce overall costs.

Digital transformation has its implications both for the supply side as well as the demand side. On the demand side, it facilitates communication and information flow. On the supply side, it enables contactless experiences—checking-in, checking-out, opening the room, taking care of customer requirements, and improving health and hygiene. The possibilities are endless. While the primary objective of technology will be to build consumer confidence, it will also bring in benefits like flexibility in operations, providing agility to respond to market trends, customisation and personalisation, perhaps greater access to consumer data, which can be used for a stronger relationship, feedback on services, and loyalty initiatives. In the long run, it will increase productivity and reduce costs. While the digital switch provides the benefit of making available consumer data and online payment gateways, consumer confidence will be bolstered by assurances of personal data confidentiality, cybersecurity and protection against fraud.

Technical revolution holds the promise of the future and can have enormous implications for Sustainable Development as well. As the UNCTAD report points out, technologies are not deterministic. The results both good and bad, that the hospitality industry can derive, depend a lot on the leadership and the management. Technology is used to serve a purpose. It serves the specific goals of each enterprise using it. And these goals are not uniform. The efficacy of the technology used in an organisation depends on the people using the technology. Dobbs refers to some key areas of management approach that can determine the transformation. First, the leadership from top that's able to see and set the institutional path. Second, continuous learning and curiosity—as management guru Tom Peters puts it, "to be students like never before". Third, building a team which believes in the ethos and can play the role of catalysts. Fourth, agility of the management, the ability to respond quickly to unfolding changes in the external environments and seize the opportunities. Fifth, the capacity to take care of the hazards ahead, but be more alert to the opportunities, to be in place when things happen, will make all the difference.

35

HOSPITALITY PROMOTING INCLUSIVE GROWTH

As the G-20 activities gather momentum there is much enthusiasm about India's growing economic power. Many economists believe that becoming a $20 trillion economy with $10,000 per capita income by 2047 is within India's reach.. In this enthusiasm it will be best not to forget the importance of bridging the inequality gap and the role that tourism and hospitality can play in inclusive growth. In that context it is refreshing that the finance minister started the reference to tourism by mentioning the role in creation of jobs and entrepreneurship. But that is only part of the story. Way back in 1997, Antonio Savignac former Secretary General of UNWTO and former Minister of Planning and Finance in Mexico in a speech in Delhi was recounting Mexico's search for a development model. Their detailed search, permutation and combinations of various sectoral models led them to tourism. "We were amazed to find this hidden and, to us, unknown jewel but our biggest surprise, what really made it unique, was the way the product is consumed— locally. This makes tourism an incredibly agile and flexible tool for economic and social development".

The facts are known and need no repetition—that tourism is the single largest employer in the world with 334 million direct and indirect employment, with low barriers to entry contributing to all strata of society, women account for 54 percent of employment in the sector, compared to 39 percent for the global economy. In India, it's a pillar of economic development, accounting for around 10 percent of the total employment directly and millions indirectly.

The hospitality industry is alive to these potential and its role in making that happen. The industry roughed out the worst two years in its existence and is now on road to full recovery. At the peak of the pandemic, the Tbilisi Declaration of 2020 projected a design for future tourism as one for the people, the planet, and for prosperity. Hospitality industry is now consciously gravitating towards those dynamics of new tourism of sustainability, commitment to people, adoption of technology – in short responsible tourism and environmental, social, and governance (ESG) concerns. Hotel Association of India (HAI) showcase the collective efforts of the industry.

PPP is the flavour of the recent government announcements on tourism. At the macro level the industry has been at the forefront in partnership in all initiatives, global and local like the Sustainability Basics of WTTC, and the Ministry's sustainability initiatives. HAI has also framed sustainable guidelines based on the needs of the members and relevant to their functioning. These are self-regulating commitments with mechanism for identifying the felt needs, monitoring responses of the organisation, indicating fault lines and emulating good practices across the industry.

At the micro level the hotels have generally accepted the responsibility in two aspects. First, commitment to people and inclusive growth through, just to illustrate, local supply chain, encourage local crafts people, weavers, dancers, folk artistes, local chefs and so on. Second, discharging responsibilities for the principles of SDG in numerous ways—avoiding single use plastic, innovations in use of water and energy, cleaning the hills and beaches of garbage, use of renewable energy, water harvesting—the list is endless.

(HAI) has been projecting the 'Social Face' of the Indian hospitality industry projecting such good examples which are often unseen, trying to remove the misconception that the industry is elitist.

An industry composed of about 80 percent SMEs can hardly be elitist. It will be pertinent to mention a few examples of the social face of the industry.

In 1996 (the year of its inception), HAI identified a special "Green" week (starting June 5) to show its commitment to green causes. So, for over two decades, HAI member hotels have been organising activities involving hotel owners, employees, their families, hotel guests, hotel vendors, local schools and communities to celebrate and commemorate World Environment Day.

In 2014, HAI adopted WHO's World Hygiene Day to inculcate the habit of washing hands with soap and water, to ward of viral infection, among school students, marginalised sections, local orphanages, hotel vendors, guests, visitors, staff and staff families. The effort helps to create public awareness about hygiene and to promote community well-being.

For Swachh Bharat Abhiyaan, all HAI member hotels are encouraged to adopt a stretch of up to 500 meters close to the property to maintain it clean and garbage free.

These are only small illustrations of the industry's involvement and commitment to sustainable development and inclusive growth. The industry is replete with examples of pioneering initiatives by the big hotels which have won national and international acclaim. The more encouraging development is that such examples have percolated down the line encouraging the smaller players across the country and sustainable practices is slowly becoming a way of life for all.

36

SUSTAINABILITY— HOW TO SAY IT AGAIN?[33]

Sustainability is a way of life, a comprehensive whole of many activities and should not be confused with the parts. Acceptance of "responsibility" by each is the foundation of any sustainable strategy.

"Everything that needs to be said has already been said. But since no one was listening, everything must be said again."

— André Gide

This quote aptly sums up the problem of talking about sustainability. It has been much discussed, many global pronouncements have been made, the latest being the Sustainable Development Goals which provides "a shared blueprint for peace and prosperity for people and the planet, now and into the future".

No doubt sustainability has been at the centre of global concern for some time now, but this concern has been couched in terms of the "future" until Covid-19 brought the world to a grinding halt. The landmark 1987 report of the World Commission on Environment and Development, is captioned as "Our Common Future" and it defines sustainable development as "..development that meets the needs of the present without compromising the ability of the future generations to meet their own needs". Five years later in 1992 in

33. Engage, HAI, Vol. 2 Issue 5, Sep-Oct 2022.

Earth Summit in Rio, 182 governments agreed on lists of actions that were embodied in 40 chapters and 115 different programmes called Agenda 21, touted as the blueprint for a sustainable planet in the 21st century. Twenty years later the world leaders met again to review the progress only to find that there were grave unmet commitments and they framed a new blueprint still looking to the future--"the Future we want."

Perhaps the world was on denial. Eight years after Rio, when 60,000 activists, heads of government, policy planners and academicians met in Johannesburg to talk about sustainable development, President Chirac exclaimed: "Awareness of our failure to act should lead us, here in Johannesburg, to global alliance for sustainable development...Our house is burning down and we are blind to it. Nature, mutilated and overexploited, can no longer regenerate and we refuse to admit it." Much later, UN Secretary General Ban Ki-moon had to remind that climate change was real and was fast approaching.

The pandemic has made the world realise, ruefully, that the Future we talked about, Is Now.

The past experience of global action for a sustainable future was marred by failure to match commitments and achievements. The review of achievements of the Millennium Development Goals (MDGs), after a decade of its launch made a dismal reading on almost all goals. In respect of biodiversity loss, *"the world has missed the 2010 target ...with potentially grave consequences." The review sadly sums up that "the window of opportunity is rapidly narrowing and the political will remains largely absent".*

There is much hope about the 17 Sustainable Development Goals (SDGs) but there is also apprehension that the cycle of gap between "the idea and the action" will continue. India has shown that given the will the world can make a change. At the Paris Climate Summit, India pledged that 40 percent of its power capacity would come from non-fossil sources by 2030. This target has been met nine years ahead of schedule.

While global goals are important it is now time for action to shift to where action starts—the individual and the community. "Together we can" the Rio Earth Summit had declared and it had visioned that the "together" action would start with Local Agenda 21. That beginning was not made and now the experience of the pandemic has driven home the lesson that the world cannot ignore the warnings anymore. Local Agenda 21 was the core of the Earth Summit. Translated into simple words, it says that while the issue of sustainability is global and should be fought together, there is no one solution for everyone, that the people should themselves work out what is good for them based on the felt needs. HAI sees its role in igniting that spark of action through its members in the far-flung corners, through small sustainable practices and initiatives which add up to an avalanche of action. HAI members have done sterling work to set examples of sustainable business practices but as the industry is composed of 80 percent SMEs, the message needs to go farther and deeper.

UNWTO, while assessing the lessons of Covid-19 that pushed global tourism back by 30 years, found sustainability to be the most unavoidable and essential component of future tourism business. UN General Assembly, in an unprecedented gesture, convened a Debate on "Putting sustainable and resilient tourism at the heart of an inclusive recovery". The tourism fraternity, in its Tbilisi declaration for sustainable recovery of tourism for the people, for the planet and for prosperity identified two specific targets:

- Shifting to a more resource-efficient and carbon-neutral tourism sector in line with the Sustainable Development Goals (SDGs) and SDG 12 in particular
- Monitoring and reporting CO^2 emissions from tourism operations and accelerating the decarbonisation of tourism operations.

Tourism and climate change have a two-way relationship. Climate is a key resource for tourism and the sector is highly sensitive to the impacts of climate change and global warming. On the other hand, tourism activities were estimated to contribute some 5 percent of global CO_2 emissions. The Davos declaration of 2007, on Climate

Change and Tourism, had provided the benchmark for global action to face the challenges, like:

- Taking leadership in implementing concrete measures (such as incentives) to mitigate climate change throughout the tourism value chain.
- Taking steps to reduce risk to travellers, operators and infrastructure due to dynamic climate variability and shift.
- Establish targets and indicators to monitor progress.
- Promote and undertake investments in energy-efficiency tourism programmes and use of renewable energy resources, to reduce the carbon footprint of the tourism sector.
- Achieve carbon-free environments by diminishing pollution through design and operations.
- Raise awareness among customers and staff on climate change impacts and engage them in response processes.

However, few fundamentals need to be kept in mind. First, sustainability is much more than climate change. Second, there is need for clarity in setting goals and using different expressions like carbon neutral, zero carbon, zero emission, carbon net zero etc. Third, sustainability is a way of life, a comprehensive whole of many activities and should not be confused with the parts. For example, eco-tourism, adventure tourism, nature tourism—are all important parts of the sustainability approach but they do not make the whole.

The World Tourism Day theme of Rethinking Tourism among others put people and planet first, highlighted the role of all the stakeholders—the government, business and the community. Acceptance of "responsibility" by each is the foundation of any sustainable strategy. One can imagine what a responsible and sustainable demand from the more than 2000 m domestic tourists can do to spread sustainable practices by the industry. There is hope in the horizon—every single consumer survey after Covid-19 has shown that majority of consumers are alive to the sustainable issues and take that into consideration while making their choices.

This issue of Engage identifies, much wider programmes for action and searches for simple solutions at the grassroot levels. Small things like use of water, electricity, renewable resources, preventing wastages when all added together can make the difference.

However, no one prescription can cover the gamut of action needed to start a safe, sustainable journey for the future. Sustainable ethos should be the credo of the industry and the rest would be taken care of by individual ingenuity, innovations and initiatives.

37

HOW CAN YOU BUY OR SALE THE SKY?[34]

"Whatever I dig of you, O Earth,
May you of that have quick replenishment!
O Purifying one, may my thrust never
Reach right unto your vital points, your heart!"

Vedic hymn.

As it signifies, the concern for sustainability is ancient. However, the progress of civilisation shows that the journey of mankind was not harmonised with concern for that significant message. The dilemma of the modern society is beautifully illustrated in the oft quoted story of the Red Indian tribal chief of the Dwanish tribe, Chief Shealth who, when requested by the then President of USA, Benjamin Pierce in 1855 to hand over their land which is now the state of Washington replied –

"How can you buy or sell the sky — the warmth of the land? The idea is strange to us. Yet we do not own the freshness of the air or the sparkle of the water. How can you buy them from us? ...Every part of this earth is sacred to my people. For all things share the same breath — the beasts, the trees, and the man. The white man does not seem to notice the air he breathes.

Like a man dying for many days, he is numb to the stench."

34. Engage, HAI, Vol. 3, Issue 5, Sep-Oct, 2023.

It required a small virus – Covid-19—to rock the world into consciousness. Public memory is short. The utter helplessness of human beings in those fateful years may soon be forgotten, but to shift away from the lessons learnt will be fatal.

The lesson at the top is loud and clear, that sustainability is the key to survival. It follows that travel and hospitality industry must accept it as a credo for future existence. The road to that end has often been described in different ways, like the early World Bank concept of Triple Bottom Line of economic, social and environmental, then ESG—economic, social and governance, and now Lifestyle for Environment. Each approach has its own strength and limitations but each in itself may fall short of the total picture. The need for a harmonious, wholesome approach to sustainability has been beautifully explained in the landmark report of the World Commission on Environment and Development, called 'Our Common Future' "Sustainable development is not a fixed state of harmony, but rather a process of change in which the exploitation of resources, the direction of investments, the orientation of technological development and institutional changes are all in harmony ...."

All post-covid economic discussions have put, along with sustainability, 'people' at the centre of any future action. The Tbilisi Declaration of the travel and tourism summit during the Covid put people first followed by the planet and prosperity as the future goals. The S of ESG – social action- revolves around people. They are good guiding principles to follow for the industry to achieve the sustainable objectives. For example, it is often stated that the social objectives of ESG cover the important supply side issues like fair wages, gender equality, social security and safety of workers etc. Such concerns for social goals should go beyond the obligation of corporate social responsibility to become integral part of business strategies. The Securities & Exchange Board of India (SEBI) has designed the Business Responsibility and Sustainability Reports (BRSR) for the top 1,000 listed companies to sensitise such industries to the ESG.

Way back in 1992 the Earth Summit in Rio had recognised that hunger and poverty are both a cause and an effect of environmental degradation. The Bruntland Commission had stated that a world in which poverty is endemic will always be prone to ecological and other catastrophes. Sustainable development is "development that meets the needs of the present without compromising the ability of the future generations to meet their own needs". For the poor, the future is meaningless, as Keynes said, in the long run we are all dead. Therefore, positive action to reduce poverty or to provide alternative economic means to the poor is an important element of sustainable strategy. In such a strategy tourism and hospitality can play a very positive role. Globally it is now well established that tourism and hospitality is an important means of inclusive development. It is more people centric than any other industry and both the multiplier and ripple effects of tourism and hospitality spread far and wide. Recent policy announcements have shown that in India too, this role of the sector is recognised.

It will be essential to harness this role through constructive PPP where the government facilitates sustainable practices, and the industry proactively pursues them as a way of life. New challenges will have to be met with new responses.

In fact, the industry can avoid such a path only at its peril. Various surveys—for example, McKinsey, WTTC, Sustainable Travel Report 2023 show that sustainable consumerism is a fore and is here to stay. 70-75 percent of global travellers surveyed were looking for sustainable travel options.

Unfortunately, the hollowness of global action is the greatest worry for the future. As the new millennium started, the MDG was launched with much hope and optimism. After a decade the review woefully stated, "the window of opportunity is rapidly narrowing and the political will remains largely absent". Then the world renewed its pledge on SDGs. There are disturbing reports that only about 13 percent of the SDGs (Sustainable Development Goals) agreed upon in 2015 have been achieved, and for about 50 percent there are no mentionable action at all. In India too, some reports say that tinkering with the Forest Conservation Act has resulted in diversion of 600000 hectares (6000 square kms) of prime forests for non-forestry use. That brings into focus the perennial problem of adjusting between development and environment and the importance of harmony in governance action. And on the threatening issue of climate change, amidst the interminable debates and discussions the only progress towards the declared goals is what the UN Secretary General describes as "climate hell".

In such a gloomy situation the commitments of the hospitality sector, its awareness of the emerging issues, its resolve to face them and its capacity to think of and pursue out of the box solutions inspires hope. This journey of sustainability is endless and there is no stoppage. Much remains to be done. The awareness and innovations must percolate down to the small and medium enterprises who are the fulcrum of the industry.

In this fast-changing world vast new vistas for the transformative power of travel and tourism have opened. MOT's (Ministry of Tourism) travel for LIFE campaign allows centre stage to Green Tourism.

John Elkington, well known for his work on corporate responsibility, in his new book Green Swans goes beyond and argues that sustainability no doubt is the essential goal, but in a world beset with myriad challenges -- technological, economic, environmental, existential—sustainability must be seen in a dynamic context. In that context business and hospitality industry's transformative role must move beyond sustainability. The industry must be resilient in is operations and regenerative in resource management and synthesise with responsible and restorative principles of Circular Economy.

"Nobody made a greater mistake than he who did nothing because he could do only a little."– Edmund Burke. Sustainability will be a reality when each proud member of the hospitality fraternity, however small, is ready to play its role in this challenging journey.

38

LET'S LEAVE NO ONE BEHIND[35]

Since domestic tourism will have to be the foundation of the new turnaround, we need to also make it sustainable, and be mindful of lifting all—the local communities, local environments and local cultures.

The world has just celebrated World Tourism Day 2021 on the theme of "Tourism for Inclusive Growth". The topic is relevant. Tourism's capacity to generate income and employment in areas bypassed by manufacturing or normal industries is well known. But tourism being the end result of so many activities, many of which are not visible, the total impact is often not seen or properly accounted for. Still, the backdrop to all the celebrations is quite grim. Tourism decreased by 95 percent and the loss to the global GDP was $4 trillion, pushing it to the level of what it was 30 years back. Worldwide, an additional 32 million, mostly women, youth and low paid workers, have been pushed into extreme poverty. According to a recent assessment made by the Ministry of Tourism through the National Council of Applied Economic Research, 2.15 crore people engaged in tourism lost their jobs.

But as UNWTO rightly points out, "it is an opportunity to look beyond tourism statistics and acknowledge that behind every number, there is a person". Unseen miseries caused by the collapse of tourism

35. Engage, HAI, Vol. 1, issue 5, Sep-Oct, 2021.

due to COVID-19 is a very human story. That faceless face is what HAI has emphasised in all its pleas to the government, requesting for urgent, focused attention to tourism's recovery to save jobs and lives. It is in consonance with the motto of the Sustainable Development Goals— "leave no one behind".

Therefore, the global call for inclusive growth through tourism is significant. It rests on two major objectives. First, to help the sector recover quickly, and second, when recovery takes place, to use tourism as a part of the national development strategy for inclusive growth. However, the recovery outlook still remains modest. Most experts believe that international tourism will return to the level of 2019 by 2023 only. In India as elsewhere, therefore, domestic tourism will have to be the foundation of tourism's revival.

Though not much recognised, domestic tourism has been the mainstay of India's tourism. The number of domestic tourist visits in 2019 was a staggering 2,322 million; the ratio of international to domestic tourist visits is 1:232. This figure includes a wide variety of destinations and types of visitors.

If domestic tourism has be a tool for inclusive growth, it will have to be more diversified and better planned than at present. The distribution of tourists, domestic and international, is rather skewed so far. The top ten states/UTs get 87.2 percent of foreign tourists and 87 percent of domestic visits. The other 26 states/UTs receive on an average 0.5 percent of arrivals. The "Dekho Apna Desh" campaign has done great service for the promotion of domestic tourism, but its reach and expanse must lift the others left behind. No doubt, the states have to play the pivotal role In making this change.

Domestic tourism can be broadly divided into three categories:

1. Very local, people visiting local fairs, festivals, temples nearby;
2. Regional, mostly limited to visits to tourist attractions within the state, or at best nearby states;
3. Visits to tourism places of national and international importance. In addition, we have to consider occasional religious congregations that attract a large number of visitors.

It will be ideal if a benchmark survey of tourism resources of the country is carried out separately, identifying places of local interest, places of purely domestic interest and places of national and international importance. The resource should include all different forms of tourism, like rural tourism, eco-tourism, adventure tourism, heritage and culture tourism, and so on. If the survey is carried out district-wise, building up such an inventory will not be difficult. The information will help in planning destinations for promotion of domestic tourism—identifying the nature of infrastructure development, finance required, agency to manage for each category, and so on. It will help in prioritising the implementation process. And most significantly, local organisations and communities can be given a role in the development of tourism.

Very rightly, the government had taken up schemes for circuits to be selected and developed. This approach requires to be strengthened with attention to a few factors. First, the places in the circuit tend to get all the attention to the exclusion of others. In an ideal planning, each major circuit can have many linked or feeder sub-circuits which will increase the options available to tourists. Similarly, the circuits often tend to be foreign tourist-centric. There should not be much difference in the nature of development of destinations between domestic and foreign tourists. There is a general feeling that quite often while planning a circuit, the nitty-gritty is not discussed with the key people who are to service them and make them economically viable—the tour operators and the travel agents.

There is merit in trying to find simple solutions in promoting tourism. India has to develop many more destinations. The new generation of tourists are money-rich and time-poor who look for unique experiences. The UNWTO has repeatedly pointed out that post-COVID, sustainability will no longer be an option, it will be a necessity.

Tourists are looking for nature and open-space experiences. And that is how India can leverage its vast unexplored regions in a way that tourists can come and enjoy a varied experience. What we need to do is to, (a) provide safety and security; (b) good connectivity to the place and within the circuit; (c) IT-friendly environment; (d) clean and hygienic accommodation; and, (e) imaginative destination development to create a good experience. As domestic tourism will be predominantly dependent on road transport, two requirements often neglected, - imaginative wayside amenities and proper road signages - should be top of the agenda.

The concept of inclusive growth demands that the community is an inseparable part of this experience—planning the tourism attractions, providing services and getting economic benefits. Above all, community participation should be for encouraging responsible tourism, which of course extends to the tourists as well. Local cuisine is a major attraction for tourists, and authentic local culinary delights should be a part of any destination planning. Similarly, culture is one of the most important aspects of Indian tourism. A survey had shown that 90-95 percent of income of artists and craftsman in prominent touristy states like Kerala and Rajasthan came from tourism. Since culture is an important draw for tourists, the destination management teams should ensure that the cultural experience provided is authentic.

UNWTO had also estimated that for almost 30 percent of tourists, shopping is a major motive for travel. India is a shopper's paradise and many tourists enjoy their shopping experiences. However, there are also innumerable instances of causing hassles in shopping, cheating in quality of products and prices, and such experiences create a poor impression. Most Indian destinations do not have authentic, branded souvenir shops that most foreign countries have. Each destination should have a system of certification for arts and crafts, like the English Heritage marks, or our own silk marks.

Just before the pandemic so rudely shook tourism, the Ministry of Tourism had drafted a Policy with the overarching theme of "Sustainable and Responsible Tourism", aiming to reach 33 million foreign arrivals and 3 billion domestic visits, building 100 smart destinations, 20 iconic destinations and setting up professional destination management organisations. As we see the first rays of hope, the vision has to be put in place firmly and resolutely in the shape of a policy. We can do it and transform from despair to resurgence. I never tire of quoting the classical poet Virgil: "They can/ Because They think they can."

39

SEIZING THE G-20 TOURISM OPPORTUNITIES[36]

A spate of seminars and discussions are probing the opportunities in the horizon, and how to take advantage of the same. It's necessary to identify the broad sectors where investment is required, and then to break up the sectors into micro segments.

G-20 scheduled meetings under India's presidency have now crossed the century, that is, the halfway mark. The way the term G-20, which was hardly known in India beyond the elite, has now entered the lexicon of the common man is incredible. The whole range of engagements are by now well known—covering government, business, people in 13 sectoral discussions in Working Groups leading to the Summit in September. Initiated in 1999 after the Asian Financial Crisis it developed, in the wake of the global economic and financial crisis of 2007, it's the "premier forum for international economic cooperation". By now both the content and the reach have expanded much beyond the original formulation as reflected in the 13 sectoral groups. Under India's presidency startups have been added. Fresh from the horrors of Covid-19, no wonder that disaster risk management will be another area of serious discussions. And

36. Engage, HAI Vol, 3. Issue 2. Mar-Apr 2023.

now in the spirit of Vasudhaiva Kutumbakam, the global south has been associated, with emphasis on what the PM has called "human centric globalisation".

A spate of seminars and discussions are probing the opportunities in the horizon and how to take advantage of the same. One long term benefit is obvious—it provides an opportunity to showcase the variety, richness of tourism attractions and the emerging economic strength of the country to establish a brand presence in key tourism markets which dominate the GDP and trade of the world, and from where 60 percent of the foreign tourists arrive in this country.

Some features of the G-20 initiatives of the Ministry of Tourism will have long-term impact on the growth of the sector. First, decentralisation of G-20 events to far corners of the country from Arunachal Pradesh in the east to the Rann of Kutch in the west has encouraged creation of infrastructure, opening up possibilities of newer destinations. In the words of Shri Arvind Singh, Secretary in the Ministry, "this is generating a local ripple of positive activity and sentiment which is promising for the tourism sector". It is to be hoped that the infrastructure created will be of durable nature. Such decentralisation may also slowly help to rectify the imbalance in tourism performance in the country with five to six states enjoying 50-60 percent of tourist arrivals. Second, the focus of this decentralisation has been on the people at the grassroots level. All the events showcase local art and craft, cuisine and culture, bringing out the richness and variety of the Indian tourism attractions, providing local income and employment and also strengthening local capacity building.

In the backdrop of a vision for one trillion-dollar tourism economy and 100 million foreign tourist arrivals by 2047, attention has naturally fallen on the huge investment requirements to make that a reality. For the first time, a Global Investors Summit to explore India as a preferred tourism investment destination has been organised. As a preliminary to the meeting, the Union Minister of Tourism held a series of wide-ranging consultations with the industry and other stakeholders. These are all very well intentioned. However, the basic issues that need attention are broadly known and it will be worthwhile to stay focussed on urgently drawing up an action programme. Some of the pertinent issues can be briefly mentioned.

First, it is necessary to clearly identify the broad sectors where investment is required and then to break up the sectors into micro segments. Thereafter projects on which investments can be made will have to be formulated. For example, it is known that much investment will be required to augment accommodation, civil aviation capacity, MICE facilities, perhaps create good adventure and leisure facilities. The need should be identified and prioritised. The prospective investors should be able to discuss specific project portfolios rather than broad generalities.

Second, the proposed investment summit is intended to showcase India as a "preferred" investment destination. The choice will depend on the overall investment ecosystem in the country in general and in the tourism sector in particular. As a corollary, the entire "ease of doing business" procedures as well as the incentives available should merit a comprehensive assessment to make them internationally competitive. It must start from what is obvious and can be done. The projected goals of tourist arrivals will require corresponding expansion of accommodation. Indian hospitality has the capacity to invest for such expansion. It has been asking for the necessary incentives like "infrastructure status" and "industry status" to encourage that investment. There is a time lag from investment to completion of the project. Some announcements before the proposed summit will be only logical and appropriate.

Third, it is understandable that while the tourism ministry is receptive to such suggestions the power for such decisions and other incentives to make investment happen lie with other ministries. Tourism ministry has identified 20 ministries which have a key role to play in total tourism development. Therefore, the "convergence" that the Finance Minister outlined in the budget speech of 2023 should be an effective procedural system sooner than later.

Fourth, it is known that foreign direct investment has also a cost in terms of remittances of capital gains. On the other hand, "atmanirbhar" has been the essence and pride of the resurgent India. It is essential to identify what areas are more suitable for foreign investment and where local investments will be preferred.

Fifth, the first stop for any investment is availability, at one place, of proper information about regulatory processes.

A portal showing real time information on schemes, procedures and programmes would be a very essential part of ease of doing business.

Sixth, as the government policy is very appropriately attuned to decentralised development, the investment opportunities will have to be spread out. Therefore, the states will have a prominent role to play. The states differ widely in capacity, resources, procedural requirements and so on. To develop a proper pan India investment climate, many efforts will have to go into affecting harmonisation of the enterprise among the states.

These are only some illustrative examples. Lots of things go into making a proper investment climate. "The most important stage of any enterprise," philosopher Pluto had said long back, "is the beginning". That holds good even today.

40

TOURISM AND HOSPITALITY BEYOND G-20[37]

Decked up Delhi awaits the G-20 Summit to mark the end of a year of hectic geo-political and economic meetings, confabulations, and discussions. The beginning of G-20 presidency for India in 2023 coincided with the revival of the tourism and hospitality sector after the worst period in its history. It was a time of great expectations and uncertainties and the many opportunities that G-20 promised brought a ray of hope.

Logically the benefits of G-20 could flow only in the long term. It is significant that the byline for G-20 –Vasudhaiva Kutumbakam brings out the essence of Indian hospitality tradition of 'Atithi devo bhava'. No doubt the year long activities and the Summit has seen visit of large number of dignitaries- prime ministers, presidents, heads of state, diplomats, journalists and so on. But in the totality of Indian tourism that number is not the most significant opportunity. The opportunity was in showcasing and marketing the richness and variety of India and its emerging economic power. Unlike any other time, it was a showcasing from a position of strength the authenticity of India's arrival.

In fact, properly nourished and followed up, the long-term impact can be much more ambitious. It can be built on the old motto of Indian

37. ET Hospitality World, Sep 1, 2023.

tourism— "welcome a tourist and send back a friend". Not only the G-20 has 85% of the global GDP and 75 percent of global trade, it contributes to 60 percent of foreign tourists arriving India. Indeed, the tourism marketing reach can be expanded to benefit from what was being called human centric globalisation--involvement of the global south in the G-20 meetings in India and India's presidentship of SCO. All the policy-makers and decision agents visiting India for the many meetings throughout the year could be the best long-term ambassadors for Indian tourism.

However, the 200 odd meetings and events leading to the build up of the Summit was also marked by some strategic initiatives for the future of Indian tourism. The decentralisation of G-20 events to far corners of the country from Arunachal Pradesh in the east to the Rann of Kutch in the west has encouraged creation of infrstructure, opening up vast potential of India's destinations. It is a much-needed initiative for two primary reasons. First, generally almost 50 to 60 percent of tourism arrivals and tourism earnings are confined to five to six states. Tourism being an important means of inclusive growth, it is necessary to remove this imbalance and spread the benefits more evenly to wider regions. Second, India has set a goal of 100 m foreign tourist arrivals by 2047. Domestic tourism has also been booming and propelled by rising income and GDP growth is likely to be the main driver of Indian tourism. As per a HAI study 2000 m visits in 2019 is likely to see a quantum jump to 15 billion visits. Such exponential growth in numbers will be unsustainable without planned expansion and development of destinations.

It is also heartening that the approach to opening up the variety of India has been people centric. All the events concentrated on showing local art and craft, cuisine, culture bringing out the richness and variety of the Indian tourism attractions, providing local income and employment and also strengthening local capacity building. The great challenge in the post-G-20 period will be to sustain these initiatives. Naturally the states will have to play the key role, providing a suitable policy framework, putting together an atmosphere where doing business is easy and creating a suitable climate for constructive partnership with the private sector.

Recent policy announcements have highlighted the importance of "convergence" of different stakeholders who make the composite experience of tourism unique. Ministry of Tourism has identified 20 departments and organisations which have a crucial role to play in tourism development. To sustain the momentum and enthusiasm created by the recent initiatives much needs to be done at least in two areas. First is the area of connectivity—air, rail and road. Destination development and spreading the benefits of tourism will depend on synchronisation with connectivity and in particular in convergence with the Gati Shakti programmes. Second, comprehensive plans and policies, including suitable incentives are needed to be drawn up for matching accommodation development consistent with the projected growth in tourist arrivals.

The Prime Minister has recently said that the tourism sector alone was expected to contribute Rs 20 lakh crore to the economy by 2030 and had the potential to create 13-14 crore new jobs. The attention given to tourism in the last budget speech indicates that fresh winds are blowing. To achieve its full potential and make its projected contribution to the $5 trillion economy, the Mission Tourism@2047 should start with the first step of convergent implementation.

41

INDIAN HOSPITALITY @2047[38]

Flexibility is the prime requirement of a future vision. The vision for Hospitality should, therefore, be dynamic and not just a static statement of future targets. It should have inbuilt capacity to adjust to evolving future changes and challenges.

"Would you tell me please, which way I ought to go from here?"

"That depends a great deal on ***where you want to get to***," said the Cat.

This quote from "Alice in Wonderland" hides in its simplicity a profound philosophy for organisational behaviour, a "sine qua non" for long term vision and goal. Long-term goal, however, is a difficult concept. Things change. As is often said, change is the only constant. Way back in 1989, Charles Handy had written that we were entering an "Age of Unreason" where the world was experiencing changes at such rapid pace that no future projection or prediction would hold true. The world has changed in subsequent years even much beyond what was indicated by Handy but what was described by him as the Triple I Organisation of Intelligence, Information, and Ideas, involving continuous learning, skilling and up-to-date technical expertise, are still important elements of organisational vision.

---

38. Engage, Vol. 2, Issue 4, Jul-Aug 2022.

The vision for the hospitality sector, should, therefore, be dynamic and not just a static statement of the future targets. It should have an inbuilt capacity to adjust to evolving future changes and challenges. Such flexibility is the prime requirement of a future vision.

It is essential that the hospitality sector's vision is synchronised, in a holistic approach to the future, with the vision of the national economy in general and with the tourism sector's vision, in particular.

During the turbulent days of the Covid-19 epidemic, HAI, preoccupied with concerns for survival and revival, had framed a short-term Vision for itself. It was a mixture of goals for HAI and its role in pushing the goals for the sector in general. The broader mission HAI set for itself was to make India's hospitality industry best-in-class among the world, raise the standards of hotelering and create value for India's hotel industry by adding employment and enhancing contribution to India's GDP in a sustainable way. The vision for HAI as an organisation was to create the differentiators for HAI and to position it as the "premium institution" for the hotel industry in India. Within that framework were various objectives to strengthen the voice of the industry, to create partnership with the government, and above all, strive for succor for the afflicted industry.

The government is in the process of formulating a vision India@2047 for a "future-ready India." HAI is also in the process of looking at a long-term vision for the industry in tune with the vision and goals set by the government for the tourism sector.

The draft tourism policy in circulation provides the broad contours of the government's goals and vision. The objective of all the measures outlined in the draft policy is to reimagine the future of tourism with the lessons learnt from the pandemic and transform tourist destinations to provide a world-class visitor experience, making India one of the topmost destinations for sustainable and responsible tourism. The hospitality sector is the primary agency to create such experiences for tourists. And quite naturally, the guiding principles of the draft policy are—in sync with the global experiences and understanding--sustainable, responsible and inclusive tourism. Sustainability has always been a key concern of tourism development. The experience of Covid has made it an unavoidable imperative and a grim lesson to be forgotten only at our peril.

Similarly, promotion of digitalisation, innovation and technology are emerging as key requirements of any future action. Various dimensions of this digital transformation should be built into the future business models and processes of the hospitality sector. Digital transformation of tourism will help enterprises to expand their market reach, increase growth, improve operational efficiencies, and sharpen their competitive edge, help to develop, generate data to track performance and so on.

Atmanirbhar Bharat is the most striking feature of the future-ready India, and this spirit permeates tourism aspirations too. The philosophy of a self-reliant India offers opportunities to encourage innovation, drive new business models, explore new markets, and create strong enterprises in India—enterprises that can become global forces. For many in Indian hospitality, the concept is not new. They have created strong Indian brands that are global leaders. And on this strength, the future has to be crafted for others to follow.

There is growing focus, appropriately, on skilling the manpower. To remain competitive globally, to provide excellence in services and experiences, to increase productivity, the hospitality sector will not only need to strengthen comprehensive skills, but also will need to upgrade and adapt skills continuously. This is an area in which the future vision of the hospitality sector and government initiatives should match.

It is significant that the government sees the future of tourism growth as private sector led. It is expected that if this pronouncement becomes a policy directive, new modes of collaboration will evolve. The private sector accordingly will have to, in thinking and approach, realign and redesign its role. HAI is following an approach of collaborative partnership with the government. The long-term vision that HAI formulates will greatly depend on how the government gives shape to its avowed objective of making tourism private sector led.

The industry, therefore, keenly looks forward to the government's Vision@2047 that is under discussion with the stakeholders. A 25-year vision will have to be futuristic, wide-ranging and comprehensive. It is equally important that it is practical and the goals are supported by firm and plausible action plan. The consultations have rightly centred around setting measurable targets and providing, among others, Infrastructure development, destination development, connectivity to tourist destinations, Human Resource Development and capacity-building, data-driven decision-making, leveraging technology, environment and sustainability, and so on. Much remains to be done and the list can only be illustrative. The journey should start with a detailed "gap analysis" of what is needed in each area to achieve the targets we set for ourselves–like number of tourist arrivals and what we have on ground to sustain that target.

Much of the government's future targets are in numbers of tourist arrivals. That raises, apart from the need for a "gap study", a close look at the desirability of carrying capacity assessment. Perhaps the future policy may also require a shift from quantity to quality. In the same manner much needs to be worked out about the future directions of responsible tourism. This responsibility binds all the stakeholders—the government, the industry, the community and the tourists.

Arthur C Clarke who said, "the future is not what it used to be" also said, "the future is not to be forecast, but created". Our vision is to create the future we want.

42

AND THE JOURNEY CONTINUES.....[39]

The capacity to innovate and adapt technology in all spheres of operations, and to provide leadership in sustainability will be the new challenges for Hospitality.

Twenty-five years have rolled by since few tourism and hospitality stalwarts and visionaries got together to lay the foundation of a new organisation – Hotel Association of India. The enumerated objectives for the new organisation were wide but the underlying focus was unmistakable. It was to create an identity for the industry, provide an image of the strength of Indian hospitality within and outside the country, to provide benchmark for excellence in service quality and strive collectively for achieving its due place in the country's economy. It envisaged that efficiency in operations, collaborations among the stakeholders, technology, concern for sustainability and creating skilled manpower – these would be some issues that would shape the future of the hospitality industry.

It was a significant event and to understand it we have to see this development in the context of its time. Travel is an ancient phenomenon, perhaps an integral part of the evolution of human civilisation. But the history of organised tourism is a fairly modern history. World Tourism Organisation started keeping data of international travellers only around the sixties of the last century.

39. Engage, HAI, Vol. 1, Issue 6, Nov-Dec 2021.

India started well, setting up a department of tourism in the sixties. Nehru with his oft quoted statement – "welcome a tourist and send back a friend" pointed out to the potential of tourism for international understanding. But the potential of tourism as an economic force was hardly recognised. Those were days when the reconstruction of the post-colonial economy needed foreign exchange badly and the country's balances were low. Tourism's importance lay in its capacity to earn valuable foreign exchange.

For the next two decades nothing much happened. Successive Five Year Plans ignored tourism. There was no long-term vision and three decades after planned development started in the country, in 1982, the first National Tourism Policy was adopted. It took few more years and much exhortation from the National Committee on Tourism of 1988 to recognise the importance of tourism, the need for strategic development of the sector and the key role of the private sector. In that sense the Eighth Five Year Plan (1992-97) was like a fresh wind for tourism. Among other things it suggested that "the future growth of tourism should .... be achieved mainly through private initiative."

To entrust such a role to the private sector and to build a sound and strong public private partnership, government needed a credible, cohesive voice of the private sector. The voice of hospitality sector was disparate, its collective face invisible. For example, in 1996, India received a meagre 2.3 m foreign tourists. As per the National Action Plan of 1992, the target by 1997 was 6 m tourists. But there was a tremendous shortage of accommodation. Yet there was no visible plan to encourage growth of the sector or to fill the gap through pragmatic incentives and collaborative nurturing of the sector. On the other hand, there was a gap in understanding. The hotels were seen as elitist not requiring any support.

The emergence of HAI was important because it has constantly tried and succeeded to a large extent, to bridge this gap. It has provided a platform for articulation of common problems, given a credible identity to the sector and enabled government to meaningfully pursue the idea of partnership. Over the years HAI has done a lot to create awareness about the industry and its role in the economy and in the process has been able to remove many wrong perceptions. For example, the need for creating a brand image of India was always acutely felt. Resources have been scarce and therefore government willingness to commit such resources for promotion of a brand was lacking. Even MOT rued at that time that tourism was what everyone talked about but no one cared. It is not much known that the members of HAI were in the forefront in creating a very innovative partnership with the government to float the first ever attempt at creating a brand image. They committed a percentage of their foreign exchange earnings to create a brand initially called Experience India. In the meantime the efforts of the Ministry to get proper recognition for tourism were showing results, more funds were available for promotion and the idea mooted saw germination in the game changing Incredible India campaign so brilliantly piloted by the then Joint Secretary, Amitabh Kant.

Much of what HAI has achieved over the years are in public domain. Much more however may be imperceptible. Hospitality industry is now a respectable and responsible identity, its voice is heard by the policy makers. Individual members have enhanced industry's knowledge pool by collectively sharing good practices and innovations. HAI's constant emphasis on quality in service and standards has enthused members to set a higher benchmark for the industry. During the Pandemic, the industry faced an unprecedented crisis. HAI forcefully and persistently articulated the industry's pain and grievances. It was heard with deep respect and great concern by Parliamentary Committees, by the Ministries, and by all stakeholders. HAI had very high visibility in print and electronic media. While the government response was always positive, actual action left much to be desired. Yet, HAI can say with much satisfaction that whatever results came out, it had a role in it. Government has acknowledged that issues like "industry status", "infrastructure status", putting tourism in the concurrent list etc. which HAI persistently pursued are now being actively considered. Many of the state governments have passed on much needed relief suggested by HAI.

Since 1996 tourism and hospitality have changed a lot. Covid-19 has brought in fundamental changes in both demand and supply of services and it is most likely that the future will see many significant changes. "Market of one", "experience economy", "consumer is King" are some of the buzzwords of tourism and hospitality world. Capacity to innovate and adopt and adapt technology in all spheres of operation, training and motivation of the service providers in new technology, creating consumer trust, finding new, flexible ways to respond to consumer demand, bookings and cancellations, leadership in responsible and sustainable ways—these are some of the issues that will challenge the industry. HAI has also to craft its role to facilitate the members in meeting the new challenges by informing, educating and sharing.

In the gloomy days of Covid-19, HAI had formulated its short-term vision mainly of meeting the existential crisis—Survival, Revival and Thrival. As the darkest days seem to be slowly coming to an end, HAI has a challenge like never before. The challenge is to motivate and carry all members in a robust journey of embracing the wider but uncertain horizons of a world shattered by a virus, threatened by changes in our environment and yet, a "brave new world" of technological achievements breaking all frontiers of human imagination.

43

THE FUTURE IS NOT WHAT IT USED TO BE[40]

"The future, like everything else, is no longer quite what it used to be. ... We used to consider the unknown future as a simple combination of already known things, and the new was analyzed according to its unoriginal elements. But that is ended. ... The rules of the game are changed at every throw. No calculation of probabilities is possible."

Thus, wrote the French philosopher Paul Valery in 1937. Things have moved at a much faster pace since then, and as John Naisbitt said in his book the "Global Paradox" "technology developing at an ever-accelerating rate of speed with each new technology compounding the speed and capabilities of those that came before". Even this observation was made at the end of the last century. The new millennium has only seen the pace of change further accelerate, establishing the truth of the statement that the only prediction one can make is that no prediction can be made.

In such a scenario is a long-term vision relevant? In fact, more the uncertainties are, more it is necessary to have a vision as a guiding star to the place we want to reach. The vision should show what is achievable and what needs to be done to arrive at that destination. I had written some time back that in such a volatile and dynamic world static future vision will be an anachronism. While vision should be

40. Engage, HAI, Vol. 3, Issue 4, Jul-Aug 2023.

steady, its supporting action should be open to constant review and flexibility to respond to emerging changes.

HAI's Vision 2047 for the Indian Hotel Industry puts things in that perspective. It first lays out what is possible to be achieved by 2047. The sector could directly contribute $ 1 trillion to the country's GDP and its total contribution taking into consideration all the multiplier effects could even be $1.5 trillion. This growth will most likely be propelled by exponential growth of domestic tourism to 15 billion visits and therefore the policy planning of the government and the strategy of the sector must be tuned to the nuances of this growth. The share of hospitality in total GDP growth will depend on the rate of growth of the GDP, but the Vision indicates that not only the quantum, the share of the sector is likely to go up substantially, strengthening the argument for more careful nurturing of the sector as one key pillar of national development.

The numerous factors which will determine how and whether this projected growth will materialise can be grouped into four. First is the macroeconomic atmosphere—global economic situation, national economic growth parameters etc. Second is the ecosystem and business environment, management of the supply side of the economy, ease of doing business and so on. Third crucial influence will be technology intervention and innovation. It is worth repeating a story Naisbitt had related to illustrate the encompassing power of technology. "A theologian asked the most powerful supercomputer—is there a God? The computer said it lacked the processing power to know. It asked to be connected to all the other super computers in the world. Still it did not have enough power to know. So the computer was hooked to all the main frames in the world and then all mini computers and to all personal computers. And eventually it was connected to all the computers in cars, microwaves, VCRs, digital watches and so on. The theologian asked for the final time --is there a God? And the computer replied, there is NOW".

Technology will impact on cost saving, efficiency in operations, customer relations interface, health safety, security, increase customers options and therefore increase competition and the endless possibilities will depend on human ingenuity. The effectiveness will of course depend on depth of adoption, constant innovation and skilling of the manpower to get the best out of technology.

The most important driver of the Vision will be policy support and business environment. Of late the sound bytes have been optimistic –talking of convergence, mission approach, comprehensive destination developments. All these await the important step of implementation. The hospitality sector expects that implementation plans will not ignore the commitment to develop structured, strong and meaningful partnership. In more specific terms the Vision's fulfilment will depend to a large extent on the policy support on the supply side—like infrastructure status and benefits of an industry to be passed on to hospitality.

If Covid-19 taught the world one lesson, that is, the future path will have to be sustainable. UNWTO's future vision to centres around the People, the Planet and Prosperity—where prosperity flows from concern for the other two and not the other way round. Tourism and hospitality sector, while setting its goal in terms of numbers – billions and trillions—must shift, as has been pointed out by various international bodies like OECD, the tourism policy paradigm from a growth-oriented model to an approach focused on the quality of this growth and its compatibility with the quality of life of residents.

Hospitality industry has reasons to feel optimistic on this count. First, its members particularly the bigger ones have been leading from the front with initiatives, innovations and ideas that are path breaking. Such initiatives include wide spectrum—use of plastics, energy saving, water use, reduction of wastages, empowering local communities in sustainable initiatives etc. Efforts are on to spread these initiatives to all sections of members. Second, HAI is trying to enthuse the wide range of members to adopt self-regulating mechanism for sustainable benchmark and evaluation. HAI has collaborated with the global initiative of Sustainable Basics by WTTC, has propagated the Ministry of Tourism's sustainable guidelines and also formulated industry relevant guidelines for its members. Third, the Vision 2047 incorporates 3 Zero targets —zero kilometres i.e. adopting local supply value chains to encourage inclusive growth, zero carbon emission, and zero waste generation.

"We are limited" said Khalil Gibran "not by our abilities but by our vision". HAI's Vision 2047 is a small effort to set the abilities of the sector free to soar.

44

LIFE—The Lifeline[41]

In these days of acronyms LiFE (Lifestyle For Environment) stands out for the expanse and the depth of the message it conveys in sheer simplicity. Sustainability has been talked about for long—the Vedic hymns extolled it, nations talked about it in Stockholm in 1972, the Brundtland Commission in 1987 charted a roadmap for "Our Common Future", Rio and Earth Summit and its review in 2012 talked of the "Future We Want". That is all part of history now. The Pandemic drove home the realisation that the future is now or there is no future at all.

UN's Intergovernmental Panel on Climate Change (IPCC) Report 2021, dubbed by the UN chief, as "a code red for humanity", minced no words. It makes clear that the warming we've experienced to date has made changes to many of our planetary support systems that are irreversible on timescales of centuries to millennia. Global surface temperature was 1.09ºC higher in the decade between 2011-2020 than between 1850-1900. Human influence is "very likely" (90%) the main driver of the global retreat of glaciers since the 1990s and the decrease in Arctic sea-ice. As a BBC analysis of the Report said, the clearest point it makes is about the responsibility of humanity for climate change. There's no longer any equivocating - it's us.

Way back in 2015 the then Secretary Geneal of UN, Ban Ki Moon had said climate change is real, it is fast approaching, and it

41. ET Hospitality World, April 6, 2024.

concerns all of us. The IPCC Report brings it out even more forcefully with technical data that Climate change is widespread, rapid and intensifying - and it's down to us. It appeared as if the world was in denial for too long. Perhaps it was a mistaken belief that individuals could do little, to quote Burke: "Nobody made a greater mistake than he who did nothing because he could do only a little."

LiFE aims to rectify that, and it links the future of the planet to the action of the smallest but the strongest player—the human being. In COP 26 Summit in Glasgow Prime Minister Modi appealed to the world community to make this "One-Word Movement" the foundation of One World in the context of climate. "These are subjects where each of us has to make conscious choice every day.", he said "these choices exercised by billions of people daily around the world, will take the fight against climate change, billions of steps forward every day. And I consider it as a movement on all grounds like on economic grounds, on scientific grounds, on the basis of the experiences of the past century, it meets every criterion. This is the path of self-realisation."

The International Energy Agency (IEA), a Paris-based intergovernmental global energy organisation, in its analysis of LIFE, cites many small examples of how behavioural changes can create huge impact. Its analysis shows that implementation of measures proposed under LiFE could save up to 60 percent of the emissions. It cites the interesting example of SUVs. "The rising global popularity of SUVs (which are around 25 percent less fuel efficient than a standard car) has nullified much of the reduction in emissions from growing EV [electric vehicle] sales," it says. Innumerable small things can be cited which have critical impact for emission reduction like reduction of indoor heating temperatures and the increase of indoor cooling temperatures and turning off lights and appliances when not in use.

One major part of G20 Declaration in India was the agreement on green development of which Travel for LiFE was a key component.

G 20 account for around 80 percent of world GDP, 75 percent of global trade, and 60 percent of the global population and about

70 percent of world tourism. It can help in spreading the One Word Movement for One World. Tourism and hospitality can play a great role in spreading this message and fortunately they are getting more aligned to the idea.

Tourism is mentioned by the PM as a key area for LiFE choices. Recent UNWTO/ITF research found the alarm bell ringing, tourism CO^2 emissions grew at least 60 percent from 2005 to 2016, with transport-related CO^2 causing 5 percent of global emissions in 2016. Tourism industry is generally aligned with the principles of LiFE movement. The Tbilisi Declaration of 2020 centred around the People, the Plane and Prosperity. Over 850 organisations were signatories of the **Glasgow Declaration on Climate Action in Tourism** committing to accelerate climate action, to halve emissions by 2030 and reach Net Zero as soon as possible before 2050.

Fortunately, some mega trends in tourism and hospitality are forcing the industry to be in tune with lifestyle changes. Sustainable consumerism is fast spreading, forcing more and more of the industry to adjust the supply chain to conform to the new sustainable demand. An oft quoted survey from McKinsey & Co. says 66 percent of all respondents and 75 percent of millennial respondents consider sustainability when they make a choice. Another inescapable trend – the concept of a circular economy where resources are reused and recycled is becoming the norm rather than an exception all across Indian hospitality sector and the HAI members are at the forefront of this revolution.

These are hopeful signs for the One Word movement LiFE as the lifeline for the planet's future. Yet it is worth repeating the quote of Albert Camus — "I'll tell you a big secret, mon cher. Don't wait for the Last Judgment. It takes place every day."

45

TOURISM--- "A STRANGE BEAST"?[42]

World Tourism Day 2015 was celebrated around the theme 'One Billion Tourists; One Billion Opportunities' highlighting the transformative potential of tourism. With more than one billion tourists traveling to an international destination every year, tourism had become a leading economic sector, contributing 9.8% of global GDP and representing 7% of the world's total exports. Covid 19 temporarily halted that progress, but it is again back on track and it is time to drive home the immense potential of the sector in igniting sustainable, inclusive growth.

Ever since WTO--- now UNWTO—started keeping statistics of tourism arrivals and contributions some 60 years back, tourism has always outpaced global economic growth. By 2019 tourism had become the third largest export category. There are innumerable empirical studies on tourism's contribution to economic growth. A recent one published online, on September 2022 (in PMC—PubMedCentral) concludes on the basis of data collected over 18 years from 2003 to 2020 from 105 countries that tourism has the ability to boost economic growth in all regions.

The IMF World Economic Outlook (WEO) report of 2022 is even more heartwarming. The WEO report analyses economic growth

42. Engage, Vol. 4, Issue 1, Jan-Feb 2024.

in every global region, connecting performance with key sectors, including tourism. Notably, those economies with "large travel and tourism sectors" show strong economic resilience and robust levels of economic activity. More specifically, countries where tourism represents a high percentage of GDP have recorded faster recovery from the impacts of the pandemic in comparison to economies where tourism is not a significant sector. As the report Foreword notes: "Strong demand for services has supported service-oriented economies."

The aggregate figures and macro-economic dimensions give a flavour of the importance of tourism but extent of the transformative role of tourism remains generally unseen.

Towards the end of the last century, the Ministry of Tourism had organised, a series of lectures by eminent persons, policy makers and tourism experts as part of the National Tourism Day celebrations. In the first lecture in 1998, Mr. Antonio Savignac, former Secretary General of UNWTO and former Planning and Finance Minister of Mexico beautifully related Mexico's search for a model of economic growth and how tourism invariably came up as an inescapable option for a strategy for economic development. He says "The story begins in the mid-60s....

The aim of the government was to achieve a 6 per cent average annual real rate of growth of the Gross Domestic Product (GDP).

The problem. 6 per cent growth meant an increase in production; increase in production meant increase in imports...increase in imports meant obtaining more foreign currency, to pay for increased imports....

The search: an exhaustive on-going analysis was made of all types of goods and services that could be exported: agriculture, fisheries, mining, manufactured and semi-manufactured goods, etc. All types of assumptions, combinations and projections were run through......"

Mexico found that one of the curious activities that continually kept appearing was the case of tourism which had been growing consistently and successfully without any planning or support from government.

"A strange beast" he said, "that seemed to grow like a weed, with no fertilizer, irrigation, care or attention." "We were amazed" he continued "to find this hidden and, to us, unknown jewel". Mexico's experience in tourism brings out one fundamental realization so relevant for present day India too—that if tourism largely uncared for and generally unsupported, can contribute so much what can it not do with a little bit of caring and support?

It will be pertinent to recount in simple language some of the things tourism can do which are unique to tourism and that make tourism an incredibly agile and flexible tool for economic and social development.

1. Tourism as an export product has the unique quality of being consumed at the point of production. Traditionally products, be they industrial or agricultural, consumer goods or others, regardless of where they are produced, must be shipped and delivered for their use or consumption where the purchaser or client resides.
2. Tourism in this respect is unique because the consumer must displace himself along with his money, to his destination for any of the myriad tourism products.
3. Tourism, given its enormous variety of segments, for all tastes and budgets, can truly be developed almost anywhere there is something of interest to do or enjoy. It could be developed and promoted almost anywhere.
4. It was labour intensive and, being a personal service, hard to automate or replace. It can create supplementary income in the rural areas and is particularly suitable for employment of women.
5. Tourism has very high multiplier effect on other economic activities providing jobs and income. The supply chain

sustaining tourism activities is long and diverse. Therefore, income and employment creation are extensive.

There are many empirical studies to corroborate the actual impact of tourism. A Survey by the Ministry of Tourism some time back says—"about 96% of the total income of artisan household in Kerala and 90 % in Rajasthan comes from tourism related income. The study also indicates that tourism plays a vital role in enhancing the standard of living of the artisan families....As regards Folk Artists their average per capita income during the peak season is nearly four times that in the lean season. ....Share of female employment is the highest in the lower income segment of the artisan households."

Another old study by the Ministry of Tourism brings out the direct employment generation of tourism. For every million rupees invested in 1985-86 prices, employment generation was as follows--

Sector	Jobs
Agriculture	44.7
Manufacturing	12.6
Mining and quarrying	2.6
Railways	0.9
Other transport	13.8
Tourism	47.5
(Hotel & Restaurant)	89.0

Tourism and hospitality stand out in this survey. It is almost certain that any new survey will confirm the basis of these two surveys even more strongly and perhaps the contributions will be even bigger.

Unfortunately, the "ripple effect' of tourism through the economy is not visible and the accounting systems cannot fully capture them. Therefore, the real contribution of tourism remains generally underestimated. Tourism can truly be compared with an iceberg, its tip only can be seen. World Travel and Tourism Council (WTTC) had identified about thirty activities to be at the core of tourism business of which only seven are commonly seen as shown below-

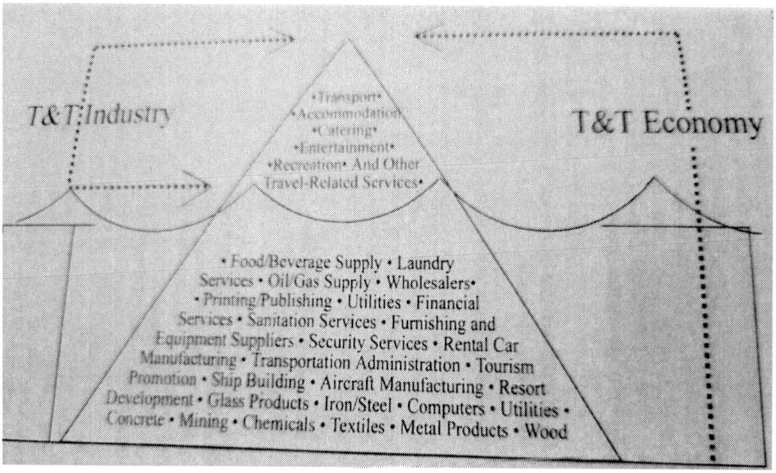

If properly nurtured there are exciting possibilities of tourism playing a pivotal role in India's 2047 Vision. When UNWTO had projected 1.6 bn international tourist arrivals by 2020---which was achieved two years before the projected date—only 7 percent of the potential travellers were actually travelling. If the global economy picks up the thread the number will grow in quick progression. India's economic growth is projected to be robust with expectation of becoming the third largest GDP in the world by 2047. Rise in income level of a larger section of people will create huge boom in tourism. This in turn is expected to drive inclusive growth. But whether that happens or how that happens will depend on how tourism is nurtured as an engine of growth.